The Path
of Silence

Translated from the French
Original title: LA VOIE DU SILENCE

Omraam Mikhaël Aïvanhov

The Path
of Silence

Collection Izvor
N° 229

EDITIONS PROSVETA

Prosveta S.A. – B.P. 12 – 83601 Fréjus Cedex (France)

ISBN 2-85566-473-X
édition originale: ISBN 2-85566-466-7

Readers will better understand certain aspects of the lectures published in the present volume if they bear in mind that the Master Omraam Mikhaël Aïvanhov's Teaching was exclusively oral and that the editors have made every effort to respect the flavour and style of each lecture.

The Master's Teaching is more than a body of doctrines : it is an organic whole, and his way of presenting it was to approach it from countless different points of view. By repeating certain aspects in a wide variety of contexts he constantly reveals a new dimension of the Whole and, at the same time, throws new light on the individual aspects and on their vital links with each other.

TABLE OF CONTENTS

1

NOISE AND SILENCE

Go into the home of any average family and what do you hear? From the moment you step into their house your ears are assailed by noise: the dogs are barking, the children are quarrelling or crying, the parents are shouting, doors are banging and the radio or television adds its voice to the din. How can people who live continually in so much noise expect to keep their nervous system from breaking down? Everywhere you go, on highways, in towns and cities, in factories and work-places, there is nothing but noise. It is becoming more and more difficult, even in the country, to find real silence. Even the skies are filled with noise! One cannot help wondering if there is any place on earth where we can still find silence.

This is why I ask you to be careful to make as little noise as possible when you come here, for our meetings. Izgrev, the Bonfin and all the other Brotherhood centres must be places in which you may find the conditions you need for a work of regeneration and spiritual renewal, conditions that you cannot find in your everyday life. So, I beg you: don't bring the noise of the outside world in with you.

I know that, to begin with, some people find this very difficult. To make as little noise as possible is not the over-riding concern of most human beings. On the contrary, they habitually talk loudly, shout and bang things about; it never occurs to them that such behaviour could be injurious to themselves and others. They manifest themselves just as they are and, having a very high opinion of themselves, they naturally expect others to put up with them. Well, let me tell you that this form of selfishness is very prejudicial to a person's evolution. You must, on the contrary, be considerate of others and not disturb them by making a noise. This consideration for others will help you to reach a higher degree of consciousness and to develop many qualities such as sensitivity, kindness, generosity and harmony. What's more, you will be the first to benefit from this attitude. You must learn to see the importance of the link between an attitude and all the other aspects of life.

Personally, I need silence. Only in silence can I find fulfilment and the conditions I need for my work. I cannot stand noise; I feel compelled to flee from it. In the presence of noise I have only one desire and that is to abandon everything and go as far from it as possible.

To be sure, those who come here for the first time are a little disconcerted by the silence. They are not used to it; they think, 'What have I landed myself in? Anyone would think we were in a monastery!' Why a monastery? Silence does not belong only to monasteries. Silence belongs to nature, to the sages and Initiates, to every sensible human being.

The more highly evolved one is the more one needs silence. If you are noisy, therefore, it is not a good sign. Many people make a noise in order to be noticed. They talk at the top of their voice, laugh raucously and disturb everybody else by arriving late at a meeting and constantly moving their chair or dropping their pen with a clatter simply in order to draw attention to themselves. To make a noise is their way of asserting themselves, of showing that they are there. But they would do well to remember that it is the empty barrels that make most noise; nobody can help noticing them! Yes, well there are a lot of people who are empty barrels; the deafening noise they make wherever they go reveals their inadequacy and mediocrity.

When I look at people I can immediately see the kind of education they have had as well as their character and temperament and the degree of evolution they have reached: their behaviour betrays it

all. They give it all away by their attitude and the
way they speak. Some people talk as though they
had something they want to cover up, as though
they feared that silence might reveal a secret that
they were trying to hide. You have barely met them
before they start telling you all kinds of things in
an attempt to give a certain impression of
themselves, of other people or of events. You will
say, 'But people talk in order to get acquainted'.
That is true but, if you really want to know someone, silence is often more eloquent than words. Yes;
you can get to know someone better by living
together in silence for a few minutes than by spend-
ing hours in idle conversation.

Noise holds human beings down in the lower
psychic regions. It prevents them from entering a
subtle world in which movement becomes easier,
vision clearer and thought more creative. To be sure,
noise is an expression of life, but not of the higher
levels of life; it betrays a flaw in the construction
or functioning of a being or an object. When an
engine or machine of some kind begins to break
down, it misfires and makes all kinds of noises. In
fact, if engineers are more and more concerned with
producing machines that run silently, it is because
they are aware that this constitutes a real improve-
ment. Silence is always a sign of perfection.

One can even say that pain is noise, a noise that
warns that something has gone wrong in our

organism. The organs of a healthy body are silent. They express themselves, of course, because they are alive; but they express themselves without noise. Silence is a sign that everything is functioning smoothly in an organism. As soon as you hear something creaking and squeaking, be careful! It is a warning of illness.

Silence is the language of perfection whereas noise is the expression of a defect or anomaly or of a life which is still unorganized and anarchical, which still needs to be tamed and elaborated. Children, for example, are noisy because they are overflowing with energy and vitality, whereas the old are silent. You will say, 'Of course, it's obvious that old people prefer silence because they have less energy; noise fatigues them'. There is certainly some truth in that, but it could also be that something has evolved within them and that it is their spirit that urges them to enter the world of silence. In order to review their lives and reflect and learn from their experience, they need this silence; it is a necessary condition for all the work of detachment, simplification and synthesis that they have to do. The quest for silence is an inner process which leads human beings to the light and to a true understanding of things.

The more adult a person becomes, the more clearly he perceives that noise is an obstacle to work whereas silence is a factor that is conducive to inspiration. Realizing this, he will seek silence in order to give his heart, soul and spirit the opportunity to manifest themselves through meditation, prayer and philosophical or artistic creation. But there are a lot of people who cannot bear silence; they are like children: they only feel comfortable in the midst of noise and animation and this proves that they still have a lot of work to do before they can have any true inner life. Even the silence of nature upsets them. When they meet other people, they immediately talk and talk as though the prospect of silence embarrassed them; they feel it as an emptiness that they must hasten to fill with their words and gestures. Actually, this is quite normal: physical silence terrifies them because it makes them aware of their inner disorder and discord. In fact, silence can actually drive people mad for, when their sensibilities are not deadened or distracted by external things, they can no longer escape from their inner demons.

Silence is an expression of peace, harmony and perfection. Someone who begins to love silence, who understands that silence gives him the conditions most conducive to psychic and spiritual activity, gradually achieves it in all that he does. Instead of creating a great fuss and bother every time he handles something or talks, works and moves about, he begins to be gentler and more considerate, his gestures are suppler and more careful; everything he does is impregnated by a quality that seems to come from another world, a world of poetry, music, dance and inspiration.

As disciples of the Teaching of the Universal White Brotherhood, you must realize that there are certain rules that you must know and respect and certain qualities that you must cultivate if you really want to manifest yourselves in this Brotherhood as living, active, luminous members. And one of these rules, one of these qualities is silence. You must learn to love silence and you must also learn to achieve silence. Otherwise, even though you may be here physically, your soul and spirit will always be somewhere else.

2

ACHIEVING INNER SILENCE

Silence is easy to achieve on the physical plane; you only have to close your doors and windows and stop up your ears. But we are not talking about this kind of silence. Physical silence is necessary, of course, indispensable in fact, because it makes possible that other silence, the inner silence of thoughts and feelings which is so much more difficult to achieve. Yes, for it is within oneself that there is so much noise, it is in one's inner sanctum that there is so much turmoil, so many explosions, so many arguments.

Unfortunately, when you try to explain to people that it would be to their advantage to achieve this inner silence they don't understand, they won't listen — even though you give them the methods they need to achieve it — and the hubbub within them is reflected in every aspect of their disordered, discordant behaviour.

You, who have come to an Initiatic school, are

here in order to learn things that are essential, otherwise there would be no point in your being here.
And one thing that is essential is to achieve inner
silence. This is why you must make an effort, every
day, to avoid the noise that builds up within you:
the arguments, revolutions and battles triggered by
the thoughts, desires and feelings that you have still
not mastered. In order to escape from this inner
hubbub you must make the effort to stop living on
the surface of reality, where you cannot help but
be exposed to all the tumult and upheavals that oc-
cur on that level, and shake off your prosaic cares
and preoccupations. Above all, you must try to
change the nature of your needs. As long as your
needs are too down-to-earth you will never be free.
Each need, each desire, each wish sets you on a particular track and each track necessarily leads to a
particular terminus. In this way, depending on the
nature of your needs, you will end up in a region
infested with wild beasts or in one that is inhabited
by celestial beings who will welcome you with a con-
cert of harmony.

The silence that you have managed to achieve
so far is not really very silent. You have often
discovered this for yourselves. You only have to
close your eyes for all your problems, preoccupations and animosities to come to the surface. In this
so-called silence, you continue to quarrel with your
wife, spank your children, get your own back on

that infuriating neighbour and try to persuade your boss to give you a raise... and you call that silence! It is not silence; it is a furious tumult!

There are people who give you the impression that you can actually hear their inner noise. Even if they keep quite still and say nothing, a deafening noise comes from them. But there are also people – too few, unfortunately – who give the impression of being wrapped in silence. Even when they talk, something silent seems to emanate from them. Yes, because silence is a quality of the inner life. But you will not understand what I am saying unless you have succeeded in maintaining true silence within yourself, if only for a few moments... and it is quite possible that this has never happened.

How wrong we are to think that silence necessarily means emptiness, nothingness, the absence of all activity or creation. In reality, there is more than one kind of silence: the silence of death and the silence of a higher degree of life. It is this, the silence of the higher degree of life, that concerns us here and that we must try to understand. This is not the silence of inertia; on the contrary, it is the stillness that surrounds a work of great intensity that is taking place in a climate of perfect harmony. Nor is it emptiness or absence; on the contrary, it is fullness, a fullness comparable to that experienced by two human beings who love each other very deeply and share something that cannot be expressed in words or gestures. Silence is a quality of the inner life.

In man, silence is the result of harmony on the three planes: physical, astral and mental. This means that, in order to be inwardly silent, you must try to create harmony in your physical body, in your feelings and in your thoughts. You have certainly all had the sensation of a sudden, profound silence within yourself, as though all inner tumult − that you are so accustomed to that it goes almost unnoticed − had suddenly ceased. This silence is felt as a liberation, a lightening; it is as though a load suddenly slipped from one's shoulders, as though bonds had fallen away and doors had flown open, as though one's soul, released from its prison at last, were free to expand and soar into space.

This experience comes as a free gift from Heaven without your doing anything to earn it, but that doesn't mean that you cannot try to repeat it, consciously and deliberately: you can. There are a certain number of activities or exercises, each of which has its own particular nature, its own particular colour, which can help you in this, and singing is one of them. To sing, as we do, before and after our meetings, before and after meals, produces a state of harmony, poetry and inspiration which, if we are aware and think of what we are doing, can ease our inner tensions. For you must realize that we don't sing simply for the pleasure of singing, because it makes us happy to sing. No, we sing because song creates an inner state of intense vibrations conducive to spiritual work.

After each song we pause for a moment of silence, and you must not become impatient if I prolong that pause. By their very nature, because of their mystical inspiration, the songs we sing raise our level of consciousness and the moments of silence that follow are impregnated with the purity, beauty and profound meaning of each song. We can sense, within us and all around us, the presence of currents, entities, lights. Why not take advantage of such exceptionally privileged conditions and use them consciously?

Another way in which we can grow in silence is to listen to music. This is why, for years now, I have given you the occasion to listen to masses, requiems and oratorios. Such music is an expression, a reflection of worlds beyond the reach of human passions and it has the power to snatch us up, if only for a few minutes, into those higher worlds.

It is useless to aspire to great spiritual heights if you are incapable of silencing the noisy, unruly course of your thoughts and feelings, for it is this that prevents you from attaining true silence, the silence that heals, soothes, harmonizes and refreshes. When, at last, you succeed in achieving this silence, a certain rhythm, a certain grace is imperceptibly communicated to everything you do. You move, you touch something and it is as though your very being were made of music, of dance. And this harmonious movement communicates itself to every cell in your body and has a beneficial effect not only on you but on all those with whom you come into contact: they feel lighter, liberated and illuminated and ready to make an effort in order to experience for themselves the sensations they experience through contact with you.

Fasting can also be a method for restoring inner silence. In fact, this is why all religions have advocated fasting and, in some cases, have laid down rules about when and how to fast. When you fast you put a stop to the functioning of certain factories within you and this stoppage induces a great peace in all your cells. But before peace can take hold, a considerable amount of cleansing has to be done and the cleansing process is often accompanied by noise: your heart beats faster, your temples throb, there is a singing in your ears, you feel dizzy and various pains come and go all over your body. These symptoms are simply the uproar coming from the wild animals in your inner zoo, because they have been deprived of their food. But it is not long before they calm down and, then, you will begin to experience a deep silence, a deep sense of peace.

Fasting is a discipline that must, of course, be undertaken reasonably and with prudence so as to avoid stirring up other kinds of problems in one's physical and psychic organism. Singing or listening to music, on the other hand, is something that you can do quite safely every day. To be sure, I know very well that you don't value very highly the simple methods I recommend, precisely because they are too simple. But, one day, you will recognize their true worth and, in the meantime, try to apply them, anyway.

Devote some time — even if only a few minutes — several times a day, to replenishing your reserves of silence. Close your eyes and try to detach your thoughts from your daily preoccupations and turn them upwards, towards the summit, towards the source from which life flows out to the whole universe. Then, when you feel that the usual procession of thoughts and images has stopped running through your mind, say within yourself, 'Thank you, Lord'. 'Thanks' is the simplest of words but it is capable of melting away all tensions because, when you give thanks, you are attuning yourself to Heaven, you are breaking out of the narrow circle of self and entering into the peace of cosmic consciousness. Remain in that state of silence for as long as you can and, when you come back into yourself, you will feel that some new and very precious elements — elements of serenity, lucidity and strength — have crept into you. And, as respiration is also a very important factor of pacification and harmonization, when you say 'Thank you', try to breathe evenly and regularly: draw in a very deep breath and breathe out very slowly until there is not a drop of air in your lungs.

Get into the habit, therefore, of restoring silence within yourself several times a day. Even if you can spare only a minute or two, do so; it is already something. Also, as soon as you begin to feel troubled or uneasy, do it again, even if you find yourself out in the street. You can do this perfectly well without calling attention to yourself if you pause in front of a shop window, as though you were looking at something on display, and close your eyes for a few seconds while you try to separate yourself from your surroundings and make contact with the world of harmony and light, before going on your way again. In this way you will neutralize the negative currents that surround you. Otherwise, if you allow yourself to be demagnetized and poisoned by them, you will be paving the way for every kind of physical and psychic ailment. Slowly but surely your strength and inner balance will be destroyed, and this is the surest way to fall ill. Don't delude yourselves: however many remedies science discovers, there will always be plenty of viruses and germs, the air will always be polluted, food will always be adulterated to a greater or lesser degree and virulent psychic tensions will continue to be rampant in the world. If you don't take precautions, if you fail to ally yourself with harmony and light, you will gradually be undermined and, one day, these things will get the better of you.

Of course, the main thing, once you have achieved this silence, is to be capable of holding on to it. What point would there be in trying so hard if you let all the benefit of your efforts slip away from you immediately? Once you have succeeded in filling yourself with silence through prayer and meditation, you must guard it carefully and not let it escape again. The important thing to understand is that the aim of the spiritual life is not to try to establish contact with the world of silence and light for the space of half-an-hour or an hour a day and, then, to forget all about it and slip back into the usual disorder and tumult of everyday life... and to repeat the whole thing again the next day. That is quite meaningless. On the contrary, the peace and harmony that you experience in your meditations must stay with you throughout the day and impregnate everything you do.

It is time to stop behaving like children who, when they are obliged to keep quiet for a few minutes, wait impatiently to be allowed to shout and run about again. It is normal for children to feel oppressed by silence and immobility but not for you and, even though you cannot escape the agitation of everyday life, you can still try to maintain an inner silence. Do you understand what I'm saying?

Not that it is enough to understand these things: you also have to put them into practice. For many people, there is a world of difference between understanding and doing. Oh, yes, they understand, they understand; but when it comes to actually doing something it is another story. But in Initiatic Science, understanding is never separate from realization. If you are unable to put what you claim to have understood into practice, it is because you have not really understood. If you had understood you would do it. For an Initiate, to know is to be capable of doing. If you cannot do something it means that you don't really know it; your knowledge still lacks the elements that would make realization possible.

The realization of inner silence is an indication of a person's degree of evolution. Only those who, thanks to their knowledge of Initiatic truths have brought order into their inner life, are capable of true silence. And not only does this silence open the gates of illumination for them but they themselves become a well-spring of blessings for all mankind.

3

LEAVE YOUR CARES AT THE DOOR

Take advantage of our moments of silence to try to detach your thoughts progressively from the pre-occupations of your daily lives and set them free to concentrate on divine ideas and images. Of course, I know that this is difficult. The ever-present problems of life have to be solved. You cannot just walk away from your cares: your family and friends, your job and your house, your money problems, etc. As soon as you close your eyes, all these queries, doubts, worries, sorrows and regrets crowd in on you. But you must not let them take possession of you completely. You must make an effort to free yourself, if only for a few minutes, and experience another kind of life.

Before entering a Mosque, Muslims take off their shoes and leave them at the door, and this is what you should do with your worries and cares: leave them outside for a little while so that you can enter into silence. There is nothing to stop you from

picking them up again on your way out, if you feel
you must. I get the impression that some people
could not survive without their worries; life would
not be worth living if they could not torture themselves about something, if they were not constantly
being fried in boiling oil! Well, they need not fear;
there will always be plenty of things to agonize about
but, surely to goodness, they could try to forget
them from time to time!

There is no understanding human beings! A lot
of people come to the Bonfin for the conventions
and, when some of them have been here for a
few days, I can see their faces getting longer and
longer. When I ask them what is troubling them,
they say, 'It's not normal here. It's just not normal!' 'What isn't normal?' I ask. 'The life you
live here.' 'Ah? Why do you say that? What's
abnormal about it?' 'It's just too peaceful; too quiet
and beautiful. I'm not used to such a life!' And
there you are: human beings are so used to living
in a state of torment that, when they have the
opportunity to live in peace for a few days, they
find it abnormal. They think that life necessarily
consists of hostility, worries and misunderstandings.
In fact, this attitude is so prevalent that when some
terrible tragedy or conflict strikes them: they say,
'Well, that's life!' But that is precisely where they
are wrong. That is not life! It is only one level of
life, and a very inferior level at that; it is not true

life. Nobody knows what true life is. And if nobody knows what true life is, it is because nobody understands that they themselves have a lot of work to do before they are capable of savouring its beauty, purity and light.

In every civilization and in every age there have been a few rare beings who were able to perceive and savour the qualities that belong to the higher levels of life. During their lifetime, these beings described what they had perceived to others and they also left certain rules and precepts so that those who aspired to attain the same perception might do so. And the very first rule is the rule of detachment. Yes, quite simply, to be detached. You must not accept that it is normal to be constantly on edge, constantly worried and depressed. It is the fault of human beings if life is so noisy and disorganized, so chaotic and distressing. If you could question Cosmic Intelligence about how It envisages life and the kind of life It has in store for you, if you could glimpse that life for yourself, you would see that it is more marvellous than anything you can imagine. It is human beings who, in the course of the centuries, have distorted, massacred and trampled on the life that their Creator gave them. And they are still doing so! Everything is organized in such a way that human beings are increasingly oppressed and over-burdened because they are subjected to more and

more temptations. Money, prestige, glory, power
and great possessions are very heavy burdens and
human beings end by being crushed under their
weight.

This is why it is useful to take a few quiet days of
reflection and get away from one's cares and preoccupations. Perhaps you will say, 'Yes, but we
won't solve our problems if we keep trying to get
away from them.' Well, that is where you are
wrong! On the contrary, you cannot solve your
problems if you are obsessed by them; in fact, this
is often the best way to perpetuate them. I assure
you, if you never manage to solve your problems,
it is because, instead of detaching yourself and
forgetting about them from time to time, you are
so enamoured of them that you spend your time
hugging them to you, caressing and nourishing
them. While they grow strong and fat by feeding
on your substance, you become more and more
debilitated.

So, try to forget all your cares for a few minutes.
In doing so you will be giving your cells a chance to
catch their breath and arm themselves so as to be
capable of ridding your system of the poisons gener-
ated by your cares. Constant anxiety and worry have
a highly toxic effect and cause the blood stream to
become charged with impurities: if your body is to
have a chance of getting rid of these impurities, your
cells must be given some respite. They will not have

time to cleanse your system if they are constantly under attack. I assure you, this is true! When are you going to make up your minds to let go of your burdens and give all those invisible friends, all those Heavenly workers a chance to repair and readjust and reorganize things? You are always so attached to your anxieties and woes; you stick to them through thick and thin. What love! Or, rather, what glue! And there seems to be no way of getting you unstuck!

From now on, try to make the most of our moments of silence to leave your thoughts and feelings alone. Of course, your inner workers never stop their work of organization and harmonization but, if there is never any quietness or peace within you, if you are never truly silent, their work is constantly hindered. Before anything else, silence must be restful; it must provide a break, a respite from all the negative conditions that obstruct the work of the Heavenly entities within you.

Put all your cares aside, therefore; leave them in a corner and forget about them and, before long, thanks to your inner work, you will be given the light you need to find the solutions you are looking for. It is often said that a difficult problem is more easily solved if you 'sleep on it'. This is perfectly true: you forget everything while you are asleep and that allows your subconscious to get the problem into perspective and find a solution to it. So why not try to do the same thing consciously, if only for one hour? Yes, for the space of an hour, leave your cares at the door as though you were taking off your shoes, and enter into the silence of your inner sanctum.

4

MAKE YOUR MEALS
AN EXERCISE IN SILENCE

People complain increasingly that the pace of life is becoming impossibly hectic, that the air we breathe is more and more polluted and the food we eat more and more contaminated by toxic substances, etc. Well, it is true that there is much to complain about! Life is difficult and often exhausting. But you must not always put the blame on life; you yourselves are often to blame for the state you are in. For example, people fail to see that many of their problems come from the way they eat and the conditions in which they eat. In fact, this is one area in which there are a great many things that need to be put right. I have told you this time and again: it is not so much what you eat that is important; it is your state of mind while you are eating and your attitude towards your food.

What are we doing when we eat? We are providing our system with materials which it will use to build not only our physical body but also our subtle bodies. And this is something that we do every day, several times a day. It is extremely important, therefore, to carry out this act in a state of peace and harmony, and this state of peace and harmony can only be achieved by means of prayer and meditation. This is why I insist so much on the importance of our meditations before meals. I know that it is not something one meets with very often. Nowhere else in the world, perhaps, will you see people who remain in silence for such a long time before eating. Most people don't even say grace; they pounce on their food and gulp it down, all the while talking and quarrelling and making a great clatter with their utensils and, because of this, they get very little benefit from it. They absorb only the coarsest elements contained in their food; they have no inkling and no appreciation of all the subtle, etheric elements it contains.

To be properly nourished, it is essential to eat in harmonious conditions. This is why we sing before the meditation that precedes our meals, in order to prepare the silence in which we shall be eating. The singing soothes and harmonizes us. People are often worried and in a highly nervous state when they come to a meal and it is very bad to start eating in such conditions. Even if you eat in silence, your inner turmoil will continue. Meditation can help to calm you down, to be sure, but singing can be even more effective, because the harmony you express in song has to come from within yourselves and it sets up an inner vibratory state from which you are the first to benefit.

However, meditation, singing and prayer are not the only conditions required in order to nourish oneself correctly: the whole meal must be eaten in silence. You must not only refrain from talking, you must also be careful not to make a noise with your utensils. This is important. If you make a noise you will disturb others. Even if they don't complain or even really notice it, the clatter of knives and forks does not give those who are eating with you the conditions they need. The brother or sister who is sitting next to you may be on the point of finding a solution to some problem or of receiving a particular grace from Heaven. You must take care not to disturb them and prevent them from benefiting from this moment. We cannot know which of our brothers and sisters the Spirit will choose to visit or who is worthy to receive His visit, so we must have the humility to leave them free to communicate with Him.

To refrain from making a noise supposes, first of all, that you notice what is on the table in front of you and the exact whereabouts of the different objects in relation to each other and, secondly, that you exercise sufficient control over your gestures to be able to handle them noiselessly and without dropping them. When you want to pour yourself a glass of water, for instance, you must judge the position of your glass and the jug accurately so that they don't hit your plate or some other object. Yes, I know: these seem to be such unimportant details and yet, if you take them seriously, all your gestures will one day be imbued with such freedom that your whole body will give the impression that it is dancing. There are people like that, you know: their gestures are not studied, they never strike a pose and yet, when they move or touch something, their whole being seems to dance.

As for those who refuse to take these details seriously, I can only say that their vision of reality is defective, for exercises of attention and control of this kind affect far more than one's meals; they have repercussions in all one's daily activities. In fact, in some circumstances, they could well save a person's life. If people were a little more aware, a little more attentive and in control of themselves, they would have far fewer accidents at work and, especially, on the roads.

You only have to look at the number of road accidents that kill or maim thousands of people every year. Drivers are protected by so many rules and regulations that there should never be any accidents. If there are so many, it is because people are simply not in the habit of behaving with prudence and intelligence in their everyday lives or of paying attention to the people and objects around them. When they take their car out they drive recklessly and without regard for others, as though there were no one else on the roads. Is it raining? Is it foggy? That doesn't matter; they continue to drive just as fast. Are there trees, ditches or walls lining the road? They don't even think about it because they have never learned to pay attention to what is in front or behind or to the left or right of them or how far away things are. Well, meals offer an occasion to learn precisely these things. And it is an occasion that repeats itself every day, several times a day. If you use this occasion to practise handling things deftly and noiselessly you will acquire the attention and control that are so indispensable in life, both for yourself and for those around you.

And this is not all: the skill that you acquire in this way will not only help you to control your gestures, it can also help you to control your tongue and the way you react towards those you live and work with. Also, when you become more tactful and more aware of other people's feelings, you will be less likely to blunder and, consequently, have to spend less time regretting or repairing your blunders; you will have a constructive influence all around you.

When the gesture with which you move an object is harmonious, it triggers forces that have a beneficial effect both within yourself and, eventu-

ally, in those around you. If you are interested in
magic, therefore, there is no need to search out ancient rituals or books of magic spells; it is there,
to hand, in every one of your gestures. The day you
succeed in gaining perfect control of your gestures
you will be an authentic white magician. True magic
consists, first of all, of acquiring control not of
others but of oneself, and it is built on the smallest
and most insignificant gestures of everyday life. If
you don't begin by learning to control your own
gestures you will never know anything about white
magic. Conversely, you may be sure that you will
constantly be in danger of working black magic. So,
I warn you: be on your guard, for you will always
be the first to feel the effects of your gestures —
whether good or evil — even if you were not fully
aware of what you were doing.

If you manage to become more and more in control of your gestures, feelings and thoughts you will
eventually change your very destiny, for this is
precisely what determines our destiny: the degree
of control that we are capable of exercising over
everything we do. This is what characterizes a
Master: the fact that he has acquired perfect control of himself on the physical, astral and mental
planes. And this is why the forces of nature obey
him; this is why the spirits and even animals, plants
and stones obey him, for he has acquired true
mastery, true royalty.

But let's get back to the question of nutrition. Once you acquire the habit of eating in silence you will soon notice great changes. After meals, for instance, you will feel full of energy simply because you have accepted the discipline of controlling your gestures and refraining from talking. And your mind will also feel freer because, when you repress the urge to talk, your mental powers are strengthened.

At the moment, of course, none of this is perfect: even if you don't actually talk during meals, your inner attitude is much the same as it would be if you never drew breath. You spend your time brooding on all your worries and grievances and do no positive work on yourself. Silence is a condition that prepares the way for the work you have to do; it is not the work itself. The real work is to concentrate freely on the infinite goodness of God Who has put such tremendous benefits into food. You still eat in silence for my sake, because I have asked you to do so, but your thoughts are elsewhere. You are not thinking of what you are doing; I can see that your mind doesn't want to work in this way so it raises all kinds of obstacles. Well, it is very kind of you to want to give me pleasure, but you must adopt this way of eating for your own sakes; not for mine. So far, therefore, you have still not achieved the most important aspect.

Food contains forces and materials that come

not only from earth but from the entire universe. Nutrients, vegetables and fruit, are energies which have materialized in exactly the same way as the spirit of a child materializes in its mother's womb. A human being is, first and foremost, a spirit but, in order to live and act on earth, it has to incarnate. It can do nothing on the material plane if it does not possess a physical body. And the same is true both of animals and plants: they too are entities − although they are obviously not as highly evolved as the spirit of man − and they too have incarnated on earth. When we eat we are nourishing ourselves on the bodies of these entities which are impregnated with their subtle qualities. Food, as you can see, therefore, is far more than you ever imagined. During the winter months we see nothing growing; the soil is bare and then, one fine day, the fields are covered with crops of cereals and vegetables and the trees begin to bear fruit. Where were the elements which have suddenly made it possible for the fruits of the earth to become visible and tangible? What happens to them in winter?

The elements we absorb from our food, therefore, come to us from space, from every corner of the universe and, when they reach us, they are filled with the life of the cosmos. It is important that, in receiving them, we should be aware that they are going to form the substance of our physical and psychic body. This is why we have to be attentive to what we are doing. All the more so, in fact, because this food that is impregnated with the life of the universe can also become impregnated with our own thoughts, words and feelings. Someone who eats while he is angry, who criticizes and curses all through the meal, does not realize that he is impregnating his food with poisonous particles and that, by eating it, he is poisoning himself. And it is not enough simply to refrain from talking: if you harbour venomous, hostile thoughts and feelings about others while you are eating, the results will be equally negative.

In order to receive all the benefits contained in your food, you must impregnate it with elements of light and eternity and this is where thought must come into play. During meals, therefore, you must try to free your mind of every other thought, even the thought of silence itself. You should not even have to think about not talking or making a noise. You should be completely free to pay attention only to your food and irradiate it with your love. Only in this way can the separation between matter and energy take place: the matter disintegrates while the energy is absorbed and becomes available to you.

Nutrition is nothing less than a process by which matter is disintegrated. Millions of years before physicists succeeded in splitting the atom in their laboratories, human beings were doing it every day within themselves. The only difference between atomic fission and the process of nutrition is the quantity of matter involved. To eat is to learn to disintegrate matter and distribute the energy thus obtained to the organs of one's physical body: the lungs, heart and brain, etc. The work of chewing one's food slowly and for a long time is the first stage in this process of disintegration. The second stage is the mental work by which our thought, like a powerful ray, probes the matter of the food and releases its subtler energies so that they may be used to sustain the work of the soul and spirit.

In order to nourish the virtues of purity, kindness, wisdom and so on, we need certain specific energies. There is nothing unusual in this: each kind of activity requires a specific kind of energy. Manual work requires one kind of energy; intellectual work, study and concentration, requires another, and spiritual work yet another. And it is precisely in the midst of silence that we can obtain the subtlest psychic energies we need for our spiritual work.

We have within us highly qualified chemists whose job it is to gather and allocate the elements we need to carry out all our different tasks. But we have to begin by acknowledging the existence of these chemists and by cultivating an attitude of real respect for them, for it is they who hold the secret of the vital energies; it is they who know how to distribute these energies to the different centres so that they may be properly nourished and in good working order. When this work of distribution is done properly and each centre receives the nourishment it needs, everything else functions as it should.

In order to obtain subtler energies from our food than those that can be obtained by our digestive system alone, therefore, we have to learn to eat in silence. But also, and above all, we have to learn to eat with love. It is love that enables you to extract from your food an energy capable of rising to the higher planes of your being and to use this energy for a spiritual work so that your psychic forces work on your food and transform it into purity, light and knowledge[1].

1 For a fuller discussion of nutrition, see *Collection Izvor*, No. 204, 'The Yoga of Nutrition'.

5

SILENCE, A RESERVOIR OF ENERGIES

Nowadays, everybody feels obliged to rush through life doing everything in a great hurry, because they are told that they must produce more, sell more and buy more. This, it seems, is necessary for a healthy economy! So there you are: it is now considered normal for human beings to wear themselves out in the interests of the economy. In this way, we are building a splendid, flourishing economy whilst human beings are being devastated, harassed and worn out. Their nervous system suffers greatly from the wear and tear, and not only their nervous system: their heart, stomach and lungs also suffer. For all that frantic activity, all that production and consumption has led to the pollution of the atmosphere and, today, the seas, forests and rivers, the land and the food it produces are all poisoned. Well, in my opinion, this is not intelligent, not at all reasonable. Can a so-called 'economy' that despoils and destroys, that wastes and defiles everything, truly be called economy? No; and this is why we have to find the means to restore the balance and fill human beings with pure energies once again.

The first thing you have to do if you want to replenish your supplies of energy is to learn to halt all activity. From time to time, during the course of the day, you must take a break and stop rushing about, stop talking and keep quite still. If you never do this it is as though you left all your taps open, all your appliances switched on: before you know it there will be no more water, gas or electricity, no more reserves of energy. Immobility and silence can help to replenish these reserves. Whenever you have the opportunity, therefore, pause, close your eyes and make contact with the Source of energy and light. Within a few moments you will feel that your energies have been replenished and you will be able to get through a great deal of work without exhausting your reserves.

When we gather to pray and meditate in silence together, this is what we are doing: capturing and storing up the spiritual energies that can strengthen us and be used in our work. But, if this exercise is to be really fruitful, you must learn to remain absolutely motionless; not a sound must be heard, not the smallest rustle or creak. Firstly, because the silence must not be marred by even the slightest noise, however imperceptible and, secondly, because you are wasting energy if you are incapable of remaining absolutely motionless. Before we start meditating you can fidget as much as you like but, during the meditation, you must not make the slightest movement, otherwise you will never succeed in concentrating all your energies on your spiritual work.

You will say that you can't help moving; your legs start itching as though there were ants crawling up them. No doubt! But if you cannot even control those 'ants' how will you ever control the wild beasts you will meet in life? This is precisely the task of a disciple in an Initiatic school: to acquire the control, the self-mastery he needs in order to enter the world of silence and harmony. It is only when you achieve this that you will you feel really full of magnetic energy and strength and ready to undertake your real work. In an instant, your reservoirs will be filled, your batteries recharged.

Why don't your spiritual instruments function? Because they never receive the energies that could set them in motion. If you put water or wine instead of petrol into your car, the engine won't start; if you don't plug in your radio, you won't get any music. All our various electrical and mechanical appliances can only work if they have the particular kind of energy they need. And the same is true of our spiritual appliances: they cannot function without the pure, luminous currents of energy that we tap through our contact with the realms of silence.

Now, you must try to ensure that your efforts to achieve silence and immobility do not lead to a state of tension. All too often, silence is accompanied by a certain amount of strain; in the effort to make no noise, people are inclined to become tense and rigid. No; if you want your mind to be free to do its work, you must be perfectly calm and relaxed, and the best way to find out whether you are relaxed or not is to watch your hands. Often, when you imagine that you are perfectly calm, you will see that your hands are still taut and restless. Our hands reveal our inner state of mind more eloquently than any other part of the body. Look at how people gesticulate and wave their hands about when they talk. And, even when they are not talking, they fold and unfold their hands, twiddle their thumbs, fiddle with a pencil or a paper clip, scratch themselves or drum on the table, etc. One of the most difficult things to do is to keep one's hands perfectly still and relaxed. This is why it is a good idea to observe your own hands: if you manage to be so free from tension that even your hands are relaxed, a sense of well-being will spread through you until it reaches your solar plexus.

Of course, once we have learned to capture the energies that are to be found in silence, we also have to learn not to use them only for ourselves, but to put them to work for the good of all mankind. We must learn to send out into the world very powerful waves and currents of harmony which may be picked up by all those who vibrate in unison with this ideal of the Kingdom of God on earth so that they, too, may feel their consciousness awakening to this work.

A few years ago, some scientists had a scheme to collect sand from the desert and use it to make batteries that would be powerful enough — so they hoped — to supply several countries with all the electricity they needed. I don't know what happened to this scheme in the long run. In any case, what interests me is the analogy between the phenomena of the physical world and those of the psychic and spiritual worlds. I see human beings as so many grains of sand scattered over the floor of the desert and I know that if they united to form a battery, they could flood the world with blessings. Unfortunately, this is the very least of their preoccupations. They are far more accustomed to using their energies to oppose each other. The notion that it would be possible to unite their energies so as to produce one great force, one tremendous light which could help the whole world, never even occurs to them. In fact, if you venture to mention such a possibility, they gape at you in amazement. Well, it is time they were told that one of the most important laws they must learn is that their destiny depends on the use they make of their energies, the end to which they dedicate them.

Human beings think that they have the right to use their energies as they please, even to waste them if they so desire, but this is a very great mistake. The energies that have been entrusted to us are very precious and Cosmic Intelligence will not allow us to squander them. One day we shall have to account for the way in which we have used them: what we have spent them on, what goals and purposes we have used them for. People need to be enlightened, to be shown where their best interest is, where salvation lies. But do you think they are interested? Not a bit of it: they always have so many good excuses to justify the selfish, arbitrary things they do. If only they could get it into their heads that it is perfectly useless to hoard knowledge if they don't put any of it into practice. Whatever you explain to them, they listen and take notes; intellectually, they even understand, but they never *do* anything about it. Knowledge is important, to be sure, but the thing that really matters is the good use to which that knowledge is put.

Every time you learn a truth of Initiatic Science you must take care to put it into practice; in other words, bring your will into play. Yes, for the will is one of the most striking characteristics of a true Initiate. In fact, this is perhaps the greatest difference between Initiates and intellectuals who read books and become extremely knowledgeable but who never do anything with their knowledge... except, perhaps, pass it on to others. It is time, therefore, to begin to use your knowledge in order to improve and transform things in yourself and in the world. In any case I must warn you that, if you don't make up your own minds to do something, the upheavals and adversities of life will force you to do so. You will find yourself running desperately in all directions, tearing your hair out. Well, you will at least be doing something by tearing your hair out!

I have often explained to you that the thoughts and feelings of a collectivity form an 'egregor', which is a tremendously powerful spiritual entity. During our times of silence and thanks to the bonds of unity between us, to our common consent, our common will to work for the Kingdom of God, we too form an egregor which is nourished and strengthened by our thoughts and feelings and which works actively for the good of the whole world. Make up your minds, therefore; use your times of meditation to work for the whole world by emanating and propagating love and light and, one day, your name will be inscribed in the Book of Eternal Life.

I tell you frankly, the day will come when you will have the opportunity to analyse the different events of your life and you will be obliged to realize that the time spent with the Brotherhood in meditation, singing, prayer and silence were the most precious moments of your life. You cannot see or feel this, today, but, one day, you will see things more clearly and will understand the nature of the work you have participated in. When that day comes, you will say, 'The Lord be praised! Thank God for the grace of being allowed to share in such a glorious task!' Yes, when that day comes and you are shown the results and the full beauty of this activity, when you are allowed to see all the marvels it has wrought in the world, you will be dazzled by such splendour. This glorious work that I am asking you to take part in has already been begun by the Angels and divinities in the world above. All we on earth can hope to do is to open a door into that world and contribute our own energies so that this divine work may reach down into the world and be accomplished, also, on the physical plane.

6

THE INHABITANTS OF SILENCE

We all need silence. We particularly need the silence of nature, for that is where our roots lie: in nature. Sometimes, when one is alone in a forest or up in the mountains, one feels as though one were being carried back into a distant past, into an era in which human beings were in communion with the forces and the spirits of nature. And if the call of a bird or the sound of a waterfall is heard, it is as though these very sounds were part of the silence: rather than destroying it, they emphasize and contribute to it. For, quite often, we are not even conscious of silence; we don't notice it. It takes the sound of a twig snapping, a bird singing or a pebble falling to awaken us suddenly to an acute perception of the silence around us. Even the subdued roaring of the waves cannot destroy the profound silence of the oceans.

Many people confuse silence with solitude. That is why they are afraid of silence: they are afraid of

loneliness. The truth is, though, that silence is inhabited. If you want to ensure that you will never
be poor and lonely, seek silence, for true silence is
inhabited by countless beings. The Lord has
populated the whole of creation; in the forests,
lakes, and oceans, in the mountains and even in the
depths of the earth dwell living beings. Even fire
has its inhabitants. Yes, even the ether and the stars;
everything is inhabited.

Unfortunately, the noise of civilization, that is
gradually invading every corner of the earth, and
the increasingly materialistic and prosaic lives of
most human beings have created conditions that are
far from conducive to the presence amongst them
of entities from the invisible world. On the contrary,
these entities are forced to shun their company. Not
that they have an aversion for human beings; but
how can they stay in places that are constantly
disturbed and desecrated by men's lack of respect,
by their crudeness and violence? Is there any wonder
that these spirits are more and more inclined to
withdraw into places that are inaccessible to men?
I have already seen evidence of this for myself. In
the Yosemite National Park in the United States,
for instance, there are some 4000-year old trees. I
have seen them and they are magnificent but they
are no longer inhabited. The trees and this whole
glorious region have been abandoned by their devas
because all the tourists and holiday-makers bring

in so much noise and turmoil. In almost every tree that grows there is a living creature but here, in this park, these gigantic trees are no longer alive or expressive because they are no longer inhabited. Just as human sages escape from the noise and agitation of unconscious human beings by going off and taking refuge in the solitude of the desert, a mountain or a cave, the luminous spirits of nature take refuge in places that human beings have not yet managed to spoil. Perhaps you are thinking, 'They must be terrible weaklings if they can't put up with a little noise!' Well, you are free to think what you like.

In most mythological traditions, mountains are seen as the home of the gods. This can be understood symbolically, of course, but it is also a reality: the peaks of high mountains are antennae which put the earth in contact with Heaven. This is why they are the home of very pure and very powerful entities. When you climb a mountain, the higher you go the deeper the silence, and in this silence you discover the origin of all things, you become one with the First Cause, you are plunged into the ocean of divine light.

Nowadays, unfortunately, with the constant improvements in the means of transport, mountains have become fashionable resorts and more and more people flock to them for winter sports. They amuse themselves on the ski slopes all day and spend their evenings boasting about their skiing or climbing exploits. Instead of respecting the silence of the mountains and allowing it to influence them and lead them to the discovery of higher states of consciousness, they behave as they are accustomed to behaving everywhere else. With their bottles of wine, their hams, their cigarettes and their cacophonous music, their raucous shouts and jokes and arguments, how could any shreds of silence survive? As though there were not plenty of other places they could go to for their rowdy parties! No wonder the luminous inhabitants of these regions are driven away by such disruptive behaviour.

Nobody ever tells people that their lack of attention and respect destroys the atmosphere and distresses these invisible beings. In fact, if the commotion goes on for too long, they simply go away and find somewhere where they can enjoy true silence, somewhere that is virtually inaccessible to human beings. And this is a great pity for, when their ancient dwelling places are deserted, their mystery and their aura of sacredness is lost; the light and all the spiritual currents that impregnated them gradually fade and disappear.

Let this be quite clear, therefore: if you are not in the right frame of mind when you go for a holiday in the mountains, the invisible creatures that inhabit them will guard against you by disappearing and you will receive nothing from them. When you go home you will be as indigent and as limited as ever. In fact, even your physical health will not really benefit from your stay, because your physical health depends to a great extent on your psychic state.

What is the use of going up into the mountains if you are no purer, no stronger, no nobler and no healthier when you come down? What is the use if you have not understood that the ascension of a physical mountain symbolizes the ascension of a spiritual mountain? To climb up and then to come down... To climb up is to free yourself, little by little, from all that burdens and restricts you until you attain silence, purity, light and immensity and can feel divine order flowing into you. I hardly need to explain in detail what it means to come down again; you all understand that: it is to come back to the noise of your thoughts and feelings, to your habitual inner state of turmoil, disorder and conflict. Yes, this is just one example of how to read the great Book of Nature by learning to interpret its various manifestations.

Wherever you go, whether it be up in the mountains, in the depths of a forest, by the shores of lakes or oceans, if you want to manifest yourselves as children of God who aspire to a subtler, more luminous life, you must be conscious of the presence of the etheric inhabitants of that place. Approach them with an attitude of respect and reverence;

begin by greeting them, by expressing friendship and love for them and then ask them for their blessing. They will be so delighted with your attitude that, when they see you coming, they will prepare their gifts of peace, light and pure energy and pour them into your heart. You will feel yourself bathed in the love and delight of these spiritual beings and, when you come back into the valley or the town, you will bring all these treasures with you. And you will also bring back revelations and more open, vaster, broader ideas.

And then, of course, there is the joy you get from knowing that your attitude contributes to causing these celestial beings to stay in those regions or even to persuading others to come and dwell there. Yes, you must never forget that it is only in silence that you can prepare conditions conducive to the manifestation of divine entities. These entities need silence and they are always waiting for the rare occasions when human beings provide the conditions they need. Henceforth, therefore, learn to love this silence; try to surround yourself with an atmosphere of spiritual silence and harmony so as to prepare for the coming of powerful, luminous beings.

7

HARMONY, THE ESSENTIAL CONDITION
FOR INNER SILENCE

You will never achieve true inner silence if you don't begin by working towards inner harmony. Every day, several times a day, you must pause and look into yourself to see what is going on and, at the slightest sign of disorder or discord, take steps to put it right. If you neglect this precaution, you will find that, when you want to enter into silent meditation, all kinds of little creakings and groanings inside prevent you from doing so. It is not easy to achieve a state of true inner silence; in fact, it is extremely difficult. It can only be done if you work all day long to prepare the conditions that make it possible, and the first of these conditions is harmony.

Observe what goes on in yourself, therefore. There is nothing difficult in that. If you feel yourself becoming tense and impatient or irritable with others, don't try to find all kinds of far-fetched excuses or reasons for your irritation. There is only one reason and that is that you have allowed disharmony to seep into you; in these conditions you will never enjoy true inner silence. Many people imagine that they can have all kinds of spiritual experiences and receive revelations about the divine world without any preparation at all. No; the rules are exactly the same as those you would apply if you were conducting an experiment in physics in a laboratory: you have to ensure that certain conditions are present, measure out exactly the right quantities of the different elements, regulate the temperature, etc., etc. If all these conditions are not met, your experiment will be a failure.

Harmony is the key that opens the door to the realm of silence. Harmony on the physical plane, harmony in your feelings and harmony in your thoughts. As long as your whole being is not steeped in the word 'harmony' it is no use expecting to receive anything from Heaven; you will always be deprived of its blessings.

But I sense very strongly that, when I speak to you about harmony, you are not really interested; you fail to see how important it is. But it is more than merely important; it is essential, absolutely fundamental. Picture to yourself the beauty of an apple tree in full bloom and then imagine what would happen if you picked a branch and blew on the flowers so violently that the petals were scattered in all directions: the order and organization that made it so beautiful would be utterly destroyed. Well, this is exactly what you are doing when you give way to anger, jealousy, greed and sensuality: you are creating a draught, a gust of wind that blows your atoms and electrons in all directions. It is this disruption of your inner organization that is the cause of both your psychic and your physical ailments and that cuts you off from the spiritual world. This is why, when you have a sense of inner malaise or confusion, you must talk to the cells of your body. Speak soothingly to them, tell them to calm down, tell them that you are sending them waves of harmony and love and that they must be obedient and do their work faithfully. Never allow a negative state to take root; always try to get rid of it immediately.

Once you have created harmony within yourself you will be filled with a sense of well-being. You don't have to try to feel this: it just happens. Even if nothing special occurs to delight you, you cannot help feeling happy. And if, on the contrary, you are in a state of inner discord, you will be ill at ease and unhappy even though there seems to be no particular reason for your distress. Yes, it is self-evident: harmony is the basis of all well-being. Someone who does not live in a state of harmony will never be really happy even if he cannot put his finger on the cause of his malaise.

Unfortunately, many people cling to the stupid

misconception that, by obeying the laws of harmony, they will be allowing themselves to be enslaved. The truth is exactly the opposite: it is when one fails to conform to the laws of harmony that one becomes a slave. All those who refuse to obey these laws fall a prey to the chaotic forces unleashed in themselves and others by their disobedience. If I talk to you about the necessity of working towards harmony, it is in order to set you free. I have never had any desire to rob you of your freedom. What could I possibly do with it? My own is enough for me.

I can judge the quality of the people I meet by the aura of harmony that surrounds them. This is something that can be felt at once; I only have to see their gestures and the expression in their eyes or to hear the sound of their voice. After listening to some people you feel completely demolished, as though you had been punched in the solar plexus, whilst others have just the opposite effect: they give you a sense of ease and well-being. I always remember the voice of the Master Peter Deunov: it was very soft and its effect on us was both soothing and, at the same time, invigorating. We would come away from one of his lectures in an extraordinary state of balance and well-being. When I talk to you, I also try to create a state of harmony in you, but it is up to you to be aware of the benefits to be gained from a state of harmony and to make every effort to attain it.

The Teaching of the Universal White Brotherhood is there to help you to widen your horizons, to give you a broader view of the world and introduce you to new practices that can help you to be better, happier and healthier and to live in peace. There is no room in this school of harmony for those who refuse to understand this. Let them go somewhere else! They must realize that here, in the Brotherhood, we cultivate a collective consciousness and a sense of respect for our fellow human beings. This is why, when we are together like this, I insist first and foremost on the creation of an atmosphere of harmony, so that all those who come here may sense and understand things that could never be communicated to them by lectures or explanations.

Anyone who declares, 'I am free to do what I like and it is no concern of mine if what I do doesn't suit other people', fails to realize that this is the most dangerous of all attitudes, for it destroys all fellowship, all brotherhood. The first condition for brotherhood is for each individual to respect and even promote harmony so that others may have the best possible conditions in which to progress and evolve. When you act for the good of others in this way, you will also be acting for your own good, for you will also benefit from the climate of harmony you have helped to create. Each one of you must be conscious and vigilant and remind yourself that

if you come to meetings in a state of inner noise
and turmoil and never consider the effect that this
can have on others, it will be impossible to achieve
a harmonious ambience conducive to the presence
of Heavenly entities – and we shall all be the losers.

It is important to understand that he who works
to create harmony will be the first to benefit from
it, for he is creating the conditions that make it
possible for all that is best to come about. Disharmony, on the contrary, creates conditions that lead
to the destruction of all that is best. He who allows
disharmony to creep in is opening the door to complications and disasters. We have seen families
destroyed in this way: they had everything they
needed to be happy and successful together –
health, wealth and intelligence – until disharmony
crept into their relationships and, little by little, the
family disintegrated. Nothing could save them;
neither their intelligence nor their fortune could protect them from the disharmony that ended by
destroying everything. For this is precisely the effect that disharmony has: it leads to the disloca-
tion of the elements. And this is why, for the individual also, there is nothing more debilitating than
disharmony. Once a person allows disharmony to
enter into his thoughts, feelings and will, he is incapable of doing anything worthwhile again.

How good it would be if children were brought
up in this notion of harmony; if they were taught

how to create it and how to preserve it in themselves... and not only in themselves but all around them as well. Think what it would be like if, when you left home in the morning to go to work, you met a hundred or more people on your way who gave you a look full of light and love: can you imagine the state you would be in? Unfortunately, the reality we meet in the streets is quite different: many people look at us with no expression at all or with such an expression of hostility that we are completely demagnetized. One cannot help wondering how all these people behave when they are at home... and how their families put up with them! Why are people so sparing with their smiles, with a kind glance, with anything that could contribute to harmony? What do you think you would lose by giving something of yourself from time to time? The trouble is that you just don't know how rich you really are or how to share your wealth with others.

A human being lives within the cosmic organism; he is an integral part of it, a cell in the immense body of the universe that is known in the Cabbalah as Adam Kadmon. Whether he likes it or not, this is a fact and he can do nothing to change it: nothing he does can ever separate him from this body. From it he receives his very life and all the elements that enable him to survive: food, water, air and light. Of course, he can cut himself off from this reality to a certain extent if his consciousness has no part in it and, in this way, he can deprive himself of the life and sustenance it gives him.

But now I must tell you something that is certainly new to most of you. For hundreds and thousands of years, the education of human beings has been so badly neglected that they have never been taught a proper attitude towards nature, this cosmic body of which they are members. They are careless and ill-mannered and totally unconcerned about their behaviour or the quality of their thoughts and feelings. The result is that they create discord in the cosmic body and if this body occasionally raps them on the knuckles and teaches them a few hard lessons, it is only because it is seeking to defend itself. Yes, someone who shows no wisdom, love or respect disrupts the smooth functioning of the universal body; he is like a tumour. And what happens to a tumour? It has to be removed by the surgeon's knife. When man ceases, at last, to be a disruptive influence in the body of the universe – and not only in its physical body but in its etheric and astral bodies, also – he will enjoy health, beauty, strength, wealth and happiness. St Paul says, 'In Him we live and move and have our being': we are cells in the body of nature and the body of nature is the body of the Lord. This is why we should think every day about being in harmony with the universe and with the inhabitants of all its different regions, even if we don't actually know them, even if we don't know exactly where they are.

Human beings have succeeded in infusing some degree of harmony into their family and social organizations and even, to a certain extent, into their international relations, because they realize that it is to their advantage to do so. At least they are sufficiently intelligent and reasonable to understand that they have nothing to gain from constantly quarrelling and fighting with others. But these are purely selfish motives: they are not evidence of any real understanding of harmony. The next step is to seek harmony for its own sake, to seek harmony because you love it and need it, because you need to join your voice to the symphony of the universe. In this way you will be opening your doors to the luminous forces and entities of nature that are waiting to pour into you and make their abode in you. To harmonize oneself is to open oneself and this openness is essential for, without it, the forces of light can never suffuse your being.

Some will perhaps ask, 'But how does one open oneself?' The answer is simple: by loving. When you love, harmony immediately enters and dwells in you and throws open all your doors and windows to the blessings from Heaven that flood into you. As a matter of fact, there are two methods you can use to bring harmony into your being. The first is by means of thought: you picture yourself living in harmony with all the beings around you. The second is by means of love. The first method is good but it is neither very rapid nor very effective; it takes years and years before you can really tell yourself that you are in harmony with every being in the universe. Whereas with love it is instantaneous; you only have to say 'I love you' for harmony to reign.

To harmonize oneself is to pour affection, smiles and showers of love on the myriad creatures of light that people the heavens. To harmonize oneself is to say, 'Oh you who dwell in the immensity of creation, I love you, I understand you, I am in harmony with you'. You have still no idea of how powerful a tool your love can be. You are content to focus it on a few creatures on earth. Of course, there is nothing wrong in having loving thoughts and feelings for other human beings or in looking at them with kindness and affection; on the contrary. But, when you have done that, you still haven't done much. And you cannot even be sure that they will benefit from it. Whereas, when you send your love to the sublime entities above, although human beings will not see anything emanating from you, these entities will. They will see and receive your gifts of love with delight and repay them a hundredfold. This is a true exchange, true communion, true fusion with the Universal Soul.

Those who have known what it is to be very deeply in love think that they have experienced true life. It may well be true that they have experienced something great and very beautiful but, in reality, that beauty can only pale into insignificance in comparison with the splendours of the divine life. Yes, because the emotions involved in a human love are always tainted to some degree by egoism and sensuality; in other words they are related to one's lower nature, to one's personality, and nothing that is related to the personality can be ideal or perfect. If you want your love to soar to divine heights, you must be free and utterly detached from all selfish preoccupations, complications or motives.

The Initiates are unequivocal on this point: someone who has never worked towards achieving harmony cannot be a pupil in their schools. This is why very few of you are enrolled in an Initiatic school. You will say, 'What do you mean? We are already in this school.' Yes, many of you are physically present in this school but, spiritually, only very few have so much as set foot inside the door. When a human being has been given the right to enter the Divine School it is something that can be seen and felt: he is blessed with the harmony of Heaven.

On your violin (your physical body) are four strings: the G which represents the heart; the D which represents the intellect; the A which represents the soul and the E which represents the spirit. But how can you play anything if your instrument is not in tune? If you want to be a good violinist, capable of making beautiful music with the four strings of the heart, intellect, soul and spirit, you must remember, every day, to introduce harmony into yourself, to soak yourself in harmony, to breathe it in through every pore. When harmony has finally permeated every region of your being and tuned you like a musical instrument, the violinist who comes to make music on you will be the Divine Spirit Himself.

Harmony is the result of the union of intellect, heart, soul and spirit. When your soul fuses and becomes one with the Cosmic Spirit, you experience ecstasy. That is what ecstasy is: the flash of lightning produced by the union of a human soul with the Spirit. And the intense heat of that fiery flash burns away all your impurities and sets you free. At last, you are utterly and perfectly free. Free to float through space; free to melt into the harmony of the universe.

8

SILENCE, THE ESSENTIAL CONDITION
FOR THOUGHT

I

The true power of man is his power of thought.
You know — everyone knows — that it is thought
that rules, that makes things happen, that creates.
But thought needs certain conditions in order to
work, and one condition that is absolutely essential to thought is silence. This is something that most
people have still not understood, for what passes
for thought with them is no more than an agitation
of the intellect. They look for something to criticize
in their neighbour; they plot ways of getting rid of
a rival; they plan a political career, and they call
that thought. No! In all this they are simply allowing their instincts, desires and ambitions to play with
them. It has nothing to do with thought.

Another common misconception is to believe
that thought develops through discussion, con-
frontation and controversy. To be sure, something
is developed in this way, but it is not pure thought.
This is why meditation is such a difficult exercise

for most human beings: because they don't know
what thought really is or how to use it. They imagine that they can enter the world of silence just like
that, without any previous experience or preparation
and with a noisy instrument which can only disturb
the silence. For this is what inevitably happens: they
have never learned to master their thought, so it
makes a noise and dashes here and there, upsetting
everything as it goes.

The region of pure thought is the Causal plane,
that is to say, the higher mental plane, and the
further away it is from this lofty plane, the more
distorted and restricted thought becomes. But
human beings live on the material plane as well,
and the problems they encounter in their daily
lives make it necessary for their thought to descend to this level and put on the crude, heavy
clothes in which, naturally, it becomes unrecog-
nizable and loses its potency. Only when it is on
high is thought all-powerful. As soon as it descends
to the level of the intellect (the lower mental plane)
and the heart (the astral plane), it is smothered
in all kinds of impurities and, once deprived of
much of its virginal perfection, it loses almost
all its powers of penetration. If you want your
thought to recover all its power so that you can
meditate and make contact with Heaven, you
must rise to the Causal plane in which absolute
silence reigns.

If you observe your own behaviour carefully, you will see that, gradually, as you rise to a higher plane and come within sight of the peaks of spiritual mountains, you become more and more peaceful, divine order is restored to your being and silence floods into you, as though all your cells were suddenly in perfect harmony. In this state of peace and harmony your thought is free to wing upwards, to fly through space, to soar away in the ocean of light. Nothing can restrain the movement of its powerful wings any longer. On the other hand, the further you descend into the plains and valleys − spiritually speaking − the noisier your thoughts and feelings become and, if you try to concentrate on the Creator or the Divine Mother, for instance, you find that you are incapable of doing so. It is as though you were besieged by a pack of hounds snapping and snarling at your heels; you have to struggle to free yourself from their jaws... and sometimes you struggle in vain.

Oh, yes; you say that you meditate, but the Lord only knows whether you have managed to direct your thoughts to a higher plane in those few moments of silence. What do you meditate about? What memories, what pictures linger most often in your mind? Memories of purely earthy things: what you have eaten and drunk, how you have quarrelled or made love, etc. And, because of all this din, you never manage, for even a few minutes, to project your thoughts as far as the regions of the soul and spirit.

As long as you stagnate on the astral and lower mental planes, you will always be tense and restless; you will never achieve the silence required for spiritual work. It is the nature of your ordinary thoughts and sentiments that has this effect and it could hardly be otherwise. It is important to know the exact nature of each thing. Just as chemists study the nature and properties of the physical elements, you must study the nature and properties of the psychic elements and, in doing so, you will see that it is in the nature of egotistical, self-centred thoughts and feelings to create a state of inner tension, restlessness and disorder. However hard you try and however great your desire to meditate, you will never be able to do so until you make the effort to introduce silence into yourself.

To think is, first and foremost, to be capable of freeing oneself from one's everyday concerns in order to concentrate disinterestedly on something of a philosophical or spiritual nature. Thought must be used in order to grow in the comprehension of human nature, of the universe and of God Himself. And this comprehension cannot be acquired from books or by discussion. Only in the midst of silence can the age-old knowledge buried in the depths of our being rise, little by little, to the surface of our consciousness. Man, this microcosmic reflection of the macrocosmos, is the repository of the memory of the world. The archives of the universe — symbolically represented on the Sephirotic Tree by the Sephirah Daath, knowledge — have been put in man's keeping. Daath is the original, primeval matter that was fertilized by the breath of God at the beginning of the world. It is because matter is the very substance of Creation that it is capable of memory and, when the spirit breathes on matter, this memory stirs into wakefulness, just as the strings of an Aeolian harp begin to vibrate when they feel the touch of the wind. Silence prepares the conditions that make it possible for this primeval memory to awaken within us.

The most useful thing an Instructor can give you is a knowledge of the benefits to be gained from silence and the favourable conditions it provides for your evolution. You must try, therefore, to acquire the habit of daily periods of concentration and meditation and begin to take pleasure in them. To begin with, they can be very short, only a few minutes at a time but you can gradually prolong them until you are truly capable of entering the Heavenly regions and of working there, of touching, stirring up and moving materials and currents in every corner of the universe. For thought enables us to understand but it also enables us to act. It is more than a faculty to be used exclusively for the acquisition of knowledge :

it is the key to everything, the true magic wand, the instrument of omnipotence.

Once you have managed to free your thought from all that is liable to restrict it, therefore; once you have it well under control, you can steer it in whatever direction you choose and put it to work to order and harmonize particles and currents within yourself and throughout the world. You give your instructions, you focus on a single idea or image and continue to concentrate on it and it is this idea or image that sets to work, finds new materials and organizes them.

Let me illustrate this. You are at sea in a boat and you pick up a little stick and amuse yourself by twiddling it round and round in the water. Gradually, you create an eddy, a tiny whirlpool, and a few little twigs and corks are drawn into it and begin to spin round in circles. You go on and on, stirring round and round until, little by little, small boats and, eventually, ocean liners begin to move in circles too. And, now, let me interpret this picture. You can use your thought to create harmonious waves and currents in the etheric ocean and these waves and currents will gradually set in motion all manner of materials, entities, minds and hearts. You don't believe me? Try it for yourselves and you will see. You say that you have already tried without result. Yes, of course! Because you have tried for five minutes from time to time; no wonder

you got no results! You should have persevered.
What can you possibly hope to accomplish in five
minutes?

If, when we are all together like this, you get
into the habit of 'twiddling' the same luminous ideas
in the etheric ocean, the idea of universal brotherhood, the idea of the Kingdom of God, you will
end by setting the whole world in motion. Little by
little, people will awaken to these ideas. In fact, the
movement has already begun: people are using our
language and our ideas more and more frequently.

Blessed are those who understand how necessary
it is to leave the lower regions of thoughts and feelings behind and draw closer to the divine source,
for only there can they find the elements they need
to undertake a truly valid work and know true life.

II

You should make a constant effort to explore and become more conscious of your innate powers and possibilities and start to put them to good use. Heaven never leaves you entirely to your own resources; it always extends a helping hand, it always puts you on the right path and gives you new mines to exploit and new treasure-troves to draw on. And it is time you set to work for, when the day comes for you to leave for the next world, all the knowledge and virtues stored up in your soul and spirit will go with you and you will bring them back again, when you return for your next incarnation. Those who have never worked to acquire any spiritual qualities will go empty-handed into the next world. As we all know, we cannot take our cars or factories, clothes or jewellery with us when we leave this earth and, if we arrive naked and destitute in the next world because we have done nothing to acquire spiritual wealth while we were here, we need not expect to receive a very enthusiastic welcome. Yes, it is your own inner being that you must now learn to explore and exploit, for it contains all the most precious elements you need in order to soar and to realize your full potential.

This work can really be done only during your meditation, in silence. Once you have succeeded in driving away all the tiresome thoughts and feelings that keep cropping up and have reached a state of inner quietness and harmony, you must stay perfectly still without moving and try to suspend all thought. Let nothing stir in your mind — not a thought, not an image — as though everything had stopped functioning. Only your consciousness is awake and vigilant.

In reality, it is only the movements of your lower nature that stop functioning. Your higher nature, on the contrary, begins to vibrate and radiate so fast and with such intensity that it appears to be absolutely motionless. This is difficult to grasp, I know: you cannot really understand what I am saying. Intellectually, of course, you can understand a little but you will understand me fully only when you have actually achieved this experience.

Your higher Self will not manifest itself until your lower self makes way for it... and this is not so easy. Your lower self is not prepared to give ground without a struggle: it is always there, always gesticulating, shouting and throwing its weight about. This is why your higher Self manifests itself so rarely: it has to wait until the lower self gives in from sheer exhaustion. And, even when this happens, the victory of your higher Self is short-lived, for the lower self is indefatigable and it is soon on its feet again, ready to fight tooth and nail. So, what does your higher Self do in the meantime? Is it inactive? No, the higher Self is never idle for it collaborates in the work of the universal Spirit.

The trouble is that human beings do not know themselves; they do not know that, to the extent to which their higher Self — and they themselves — are sharers in the divine life, they also collaborate in the divine work. They cannot know what is going on in the higher spheres of their own being because they have no conscious communication with those spheres. And this is precisely what you must work at.

The Divine Spirit dwells in each one of us and if we have to put ourselves at His service it is not in order to make Him strong for He is almighty; nor is it in order to instruct Him for He is omniscient; nor is it in order to purify Him for He is a spark, a flame. The only thing we have to do is open the way for Him; when we do this He gives us His own light, peace and love. This is the work you should be doing in the silence of your meditations.

But you must also learn to bring the silence of your higher Self into your everyday life. Suppose, for instance, that you have to have a very difficult discussion with someone and that there is a danger that you will be carried away and let it degenerate into a quarrel, try to create a zone of silence within yourself and to pray. If you do this you will feel detached and shielded from irritation and spite because the conditions created by true silence are not conducive to the manifestations of the personality. In true silence the personality's hands are tied; it is paralysed.

Learn to free yourselves, therefore, and to make room for your divine nature, your divine Self. Say to it, 'All I have is yours; take possession of me and use me as you will; I am at your service.' And if some of you wonder what good that can do, let me tell you that a genuine spiritualist[1] would never ask himself such a thing. A question like that shows that one has not the slightest intuition about true science, true philosophy. When a human being decides to dedicate himself and all that he owns to the Lord he makes it possible for the divine principle to work and manifest itself through him. This is why Jesus said, 'My Father is constantly at work and I work with Him'. Jesus was in a position to

---

1 The word 'spiritualist' in the language of Omraam Mikhaël Aïvanhov denotes one who looks at things from a spiritual point of view, whose philosophy of life is based on belief in a spiritual reality.

say this because he had consecrated himself totally
to his Heavenly Father; he had allowed Him to take
complete possession of him and, because of this,
he could collaborate in His work. Jesus also said,
'I and my Father are one' which means exactly the
same thing.

And this applies to you, also: if you manage to
give your higher Self the place of honour within you,
you will already be sharing in the cosmic work of
Christ, of God Himself. Yes, this work is something
mysterious, an activity that takes place in a different
sphere, often without our knowledge. When we are
absorbed in our everyday work we don't know what
the spirit within us is doing. But perhaps, one day,
when our brain is sufficiently developed, we shall
become aware of the work that our spirit does in
the universe. For the time being, the important thing
is to renew contact with it. And it is precisely this
that must be your sole preoccupation during your
meditations: to bring peace and silence to all your
inner inhabitants and, in this stillness, to unite with
your higher Self, the quintessence of God Himself.

Just as − or even more than − you participate
in the life of your family, your town or village and
your country, you must learn to participate in the
life of the cosmos. And it is during our prayers,
meditations and songs that you can do this. As long
as you are conscious that, at these moments, you
have the conditions you need to work and achieve

something through thought, you can use them to participate actively in the life of the cosmos.

What makes you think that you have to be an astronaut and ride in a spacecraft in order to travel and work in the cosmos? The earth travels through etheric space, carried along by the impetus of the sun, and we are passengers on the spaceship earth as it voyages amongst the stars. It is this that makes us citizens of the cosmos capable of participating consciously and luminously in the life of the universe. It is time to grow out of the narrow notions that have been dinned into us by our education and by society, and to embrace broader, vaster, more grandiose conceptions; it is time to participate consciously in the cosmic work of light under the aegis of Christ.

If you took the trouble to look more deeply into the meaning of Jesus' words, 'My Father is constantly at work and I work with Him', boundless horizons would open up before your eyes. Instead of which, you prefer to leave Jesus to do all the work with his Father while you take care of your pigs and your poultry! 'But there's a world of difference between us and Jesus!' you will object; 'Jesus was the Christ; he was perfect. It would be a sin of pride to imagine that we could do the same work that he did.' Very well; think what you like, but Jesus thought differently. Not only did he say, 'Therefore you shall be perfect, just as your Father in heaven is perfect' he also said, 'He who believes in me, the works that I do he will do also; and greater works than these he will do'. This is why I say that Christians are lazy. They want us to believe that it is humility that prevents them from undertaking the only activity worthy of being undertaken by human beings, that of participating in the work of God. No; I tell you: it is not humility, it is sloth! The mentality of Christians is closer to that of the common herd than to the spirit of Christ and of the great Masters.

Like Jesus, Initiates whose consciousness is awakened participate unceasingly in God's work. And if you, too, want to have a part in it, I can give you a method. Start by keeping silence and remaining completely motionless for a long moment and, then, let yourself rise, mentally, imagining that you are gradually leaving your physical body through the opening at the top of your head. You continue to rise, through your Causal and Buddhic bodies until you reach your Atmic body and, once there, you link yourself to the Universal Soul and participate in the work that It is doing in all the regions of the world at the same time. You may not know what work you are accomplishing in this way, but your spirit knows exactly what you are doing.

9

THE QUEST FOR SILENCE IS THE QUEST FOR THE CENTRE

To refrain from making a noise is not an end in itself; it is simply a preliminary step, a necessary condition that has to be met before attaining that other silence, the inner silence which is nothing less than the harmonious accord of the numerous wills that express themselves within us. The heart, the intellect, the eyes and ears, the stomach and belly, the genitals, the arms and legs, etc., all have a will of their own. They all need and clamour for something and their individual needs are often contradictory. The only way to restore order is through the intervention of a power capable of harmonizing them and steering them in one direction for one purpose; through the intervention, in other words, of an intelligence, a head, capable of governing and organizing the whole. The cells of our organs and the entities that dwell in them obey none but the head; they recognize no other authority. Left to themselves, they do nothing but plunder and devour each other but, as it is a law of the universe that inferiors must obey and submit to their superiors, they bow to the authority of the head.

The head is an intelligent principle which possesses faculties superior to those of the organs. When the head, the supreme principle, is present, all others obey and, if the head demands order, peace and silence, not a word is heard: the feelings fall silent, even thought is silenced, consciousness alone subsists. He who has enthroned this silence within himself is in communion with the Universal Soul; he vibrates in unison with It; he understands It; he perceives It. But... it is useless to say more: the reality of what he discovers is so far beyond the power of words to describe. It is unutterable; it can only be experienced.

We must not let a day go by without making an effort to seek out this head, this Divine Intelligence, and release It from the prison in which we have been holding It. Once we have achieved this magnificent silence, there is no reason why we should not go back to work and set our heart and mind, our arms and legs – and our tongues – in motion again. But it is the head that must come first because this is the only way to ensure that everything we do will be well-inspired; that all our thoughts and desires, all our sensations and emotions, will be guided by a higher will, by the Spirit.

There is another way of explaining this question

and that is to say that silence is achieved when the life of the periphery moves in orbit around a centre. In fact, isn't this precisely why we go and contemplate the rising sun: because it is an exercise that helps us to find our own centre[1]? The sun sustains, organizes and vivifies a system of which it is the centre. If the movement of the planets in orbit around the sun is seen as the image *par excellence* of universal harmony it is for the simple reason that the planets orbit around a centre which holds everything in equilibrium. If the sun disappeared from its place at the centre, the result would be chaos. And the same is true for us: as long as we have no fixed centre to sustain, balance and coordinate the movements of the periphery, our life and work cannot be harmonious and constructive.

When you focus your attention on the sun, remember that it is within yourself, also, that you must find the centre. Contemplation of the sun can truly benefit you only if you see it as a symbol of your inner life. While you are gazing at it, therefore, you must seek your own inner centre, your own inner Spirit of wisdom, omnipotence, omniscience and universal love, and try to come ever closer to It. As long as you remain far from the centre you will be at the mercy of all the most chaotic and contradictory currents.

1 See *Complete Works*, vol. 10, 'The Splendour of Tiphareth', chaps. 1 and 2

Of course, we are constantly obliged to leave the centre in order to go and look after things at the periphery. True, but the fact that we have to move away from the centre does not mean that we have to sever our ties with it. On the contrary! The more obligations and activities you have in the world — that is to say, at the periphery — the more you must strengthen the bonds that link you to the centre, the Spirit, for it is from this centre that you receive the light, energy and peace you need to carry your undertakings through to a successful conclusion. By maintaining your bonds with it, therefore, not only will you yourself be constantly nourished, but you will become a centre for other creatures that exist at the periphery and will be able to share with them the benefits of all the good things you receive. As long as you have not understood this law you will always be miserable, always be tossed to and fro.

Some of you may say, 'But I can't just go off and look for the centre and leave my husband (or wife) alone. We are very close and we have no intention of being separated.' Very well, if you insist: stay together; never leave each other. But one fine day you will have nothing more to give each other because you will never have made any effort to renew or enrich yourself. And, when that day comes, nothing will be capable of holding you together: you will separate for good. How can human beings be made to understand that to love someone is not to glue themselves to them and never leave their side for an instant? On the contrary, anyone who wants to be sure that his love will endure knows that he has to go on a 'journey' from time to time. Call this journey what you will: prayer, meditation, contemplation, the quest for silence, for the head, for the centre, for the Source, for God... It is this that enables you to bring back gifts for those you love: your husband or wife, your children, your friends. And what are these gifts? A purer, more harmonious, more poetic life.

Time and again I have told you that you only have to observe the facts of everyday life to understand the laws that govern our inner life. What do the fathers of families in very poor countries do? They go and look for work abroad because they know that, if they stay in their own country, they will never earn enough money to feed their family. They love their family and yet they leave them; they leave them, in fact, because they love them. If they didn't leave them they would die of hunger. And what does any ordinary family man do? Every morning he leaves home and goes to work to earn the money that will enable him to provide his family with the things they need. Well, these examples should throw some light on the laws of the inner life: in every area of life, if you want to be truly useful to those around you, if you want to bring them happiness and prosperity, you have to leave them from time to time and 'go abroad'; you have to go to work, go and look for the centre, go in search of silence.

As I have said, only those who are very much in love really know what silence is. Their feeling is so strong that it fulfils them in a way that no words can express. They need only to be together without speaking to experience the utmost intensity of life. Yes, but in most cases, that kind of love doesn't last; they don't know how to make it last, and, one day, the silence between them becomes a silence of indifference, resentment, even hatred. Why? Because they have lived their love in such a selfish, narrow way. They have focused exclusively on each other, giving each other, immediately, all their most precious gifts. It never occurred to them that they should renew themselves every day and seek new riches, new light, a new beauty. This is why they end by having nothing but the dregs to offer each other, by having no more love to give each other.

When you contemplate the sun in the morning, therefore, think that, by drawing closer to the centre of our universe, you are drawing closer to your own centre. When you draw closer to the sun you become more alive because the sun is the fire of life. Every morning, as you approach the sun, tell yourself that you are going to capture just one spark, one tiny flame; that you are going to bury this flame, this precious treasure, deep down inside yourself and keep it with you always. It is thanks to this flame that your life will be purified and sublimated; wherever you go you will take purity and light with you.

We find a reflection of this inner phenomenon in a rite of the Orthodox Church: on certain Feasts — notably at Easter — each member of the congregation has a candle in his hand. At one point in the ceremony, the celebrant lights a large candle and, from it, lights the candle of the person nearest to him. He, in turn, passes on the flame to his neighbour and, in this way, the flame is communicated from one to the other until the whole church is flooded with light. And all because of one candle that has communicated its light to all the others! Symbolically, this is what we must do. When we approach the centre, the sun, we must mentally light our candle; in this way, the whole world will, one day, be illuminated. In the presence of the sun which is so bright and luminous, how can we possibly remain dark and lack-lustre?

10

SPEECH AND THE LOGOS

Try to acquire a taste for the frequent moments of silence that we observe when we are together and learn to take advantage of them to do some truly creative work of thought. Never forget that it is this mental work that matters most, for it is this that will gradually enable you to attain the ideal to which you aspire. Every day, by means of your prayers and meditations, you can add something to the edifice you are building, a brick here, a plank, a nail or some cement there. What a tremendous undertaking! And how wonderful to feel that you are achieving something, that you are forging ahead!

If you always come here with this awareness of the work you can do during our meetings, you will no longer need to wait impatiently for me to break the silence and begin speaking to you. What are words in comparison with a silence of this kind?

Speech has very limited possibilities; most of the words we use were forged by ordinary human

beings to express ordinary needs. There are a few
terms that can be used to express philosophical or
mystical realities, but very few. This is why, when
we want to communicate a spiritual experience, we
often prefer to be silent and express ourselves with
a glance or a gesture, for we sense that words are
powerless. You will say, 'Are you saying that speech
is ineffective?' No; to the extent to which speech
is one with the Logos, the Divine Word, that is to
say, to the extent to which our words are pregnant
with the life of the spirit, they are powerful and
effective. Otherwise, it is true, they cannot achieve
much; they are hollow, empty containers.

The Logos[1] belongs to the world of the spirit,
to the world of creative thought. He who thinks,
creates. When you think, you are, as it were, speaking and your silent word is magically effective: it
is the Logos. The Logos, therefore, is a word that
has not yet been brought down onto the physical
plane. It exists, it is real and alive, but it remains
inaudible and manifests itself in the invisible world
as colours, forms and resonances that are intelligible to all. Whereas speech, which expresses itself
on the physical plane and uses the words of a particular language, is intelligible only to those who
know that language. And this is where so many
problems begin.

1 For a fuller discussion of this question, see *Complete Works*,
vol. 32, chap. 11.

The universal language is the Logos. If you speak inwardly, with all your heart and soul, even plants, insects and birds, the stars and the planets will understand you because the language of the heart and soul are universally understood in nature. A truly sensitive, receptive person is capable of understanding your thoughts and desires, even if he does not speak your language: he will sense them. There are beings who are so highly evolved and so sensitive, in fact, that they can perceive a thought as soon as it is formulated. And, of course, the spirits of light, Angels, don't use words when they speak to each other — nor when they speak to us: they emit waves and it is these waves that we translate into words.

I think that this is quite clear for you, now: firstly, you think and feel; that is the Logos. Secondly, you find a form in which to clothe your thought and this form is speech, the words you use in a given language. Your skill with words may or may not allow you to express your thought adequately whereas the Logos always and instantly finds appropriate expression on the invisible plane and all created beings, even the Angels and Archangels, understand it.

Speech is often the cause of all kinds of misunderstandings because people have difficulty in finding the right words with which to express themselves. In fact, they often have no very clear idea of what they really want to say. But speech cannot be vital and potent if it is not impregnated by the Logos and does not accurately express the experience of the soul and spirit. The day will come when human beings will no longer communicate with words but with the light, colours and sounds that emanate from their very being; then they will understand each other immediately. When someone beside you is in pain, you can feel his pain even if he doesn't talk about it. And when he is full of joy, you can feel that, too. Suffering and joy are a language that has no need of words, a language that cannot lie.

The Logos is a synthesis of all the expressions of a person's inner life, of all the emanations of his thoughts and feelings and, in this sense, it is true to say that the Logos, a man's inner Word, is often in direct contradiction to his speech. How many people use speech not as a truthful reflection of reality but as a means of arousing feelings or reactions in others that are designed to serve their own purposes: to persuade people to trust them and distrust someone else, for instance.

But you must not think that I mean to underestimate the power of words. On the contrary, my purpose is to show you the conditions it requires in order to be magically effective. Thought creates things on a higher level and speech materializes them by causing particles of matter to adhere to certain lines of force. This is why speech is necessary in order to realize your thoughts and desires on the physical plane. However, before you can achieve this, there is a law that you must know. Let's use an image: the words you use are like the barrel of a gun and your thought or desire is the gunpowder. If you don't put any gunpowder in the barrel, you can take aim and pull the trigger as much as you like, but nothing will happen. On the other hand, if your gun has no barrel, you cannot aim your bullets. The barrel gives your projectile direction and the gunpowder gives it power, impetus. First, therefore, you must have potent, ardent thoughts and feelings; secondly, you must aim them in the desired direction by means of words. Psychic energy and words must be combined; both are necessary.

No, you must never underestimate the power of speech; it is extremely important, for it is through speech that we keep our inner tensions in equilibrium. When you pray and meditate in silence, you generate psychic energy and it is important to give this energy an outlet in speech. Failure to do so can cause problems: an excessive buildup of forces and tensions can become a threat to your inner equilibrium. Words can be the means, the clothes these forces need in order to manifest themselves and be effective. If you fail to give your accumulated psychic energy an outlet, it will explode and destroy you. So it is very important to project this energy and give it a goal; and this is precisely the function of speech.

Get into the habit, therefore, of using words effectively. Use your thoughts to enter into communion with the purest energies of the invisible world and, when you sense that you have achieved this, don't stop there: there is still some work to be done. Choose some brief formula, such as, 'May the Kingdom of God and His Righteousness be established on earth' or 'Thy Kingdom come on earth as it is in Heaven', and say it out loud. In this way you will be giving direction and purpose to these energies and doing a useful work for the whole of mankind. A knowledge of these laws is the foundation of all spiritual work.

When an Initiate meditates in silence, he recharges his batteries and builds up the forces within himself so that, when he speaks, his words may be pregnant and alive. Before speaking we must fill our words with love and divine power, for the origin and source of all things, the only true power, is the Logos. This is why speech must come after the Logos. The spirit must always be present and wide awake. When it is, you will have a livelier understanding of things, you will express them better and others will feel that what you say is alive.

There is one thing more that I must tell you and it is this: you must not rely exclusively on what I reveal to you on the physical plane, for it does not amount to very much. Also, I am sometimes away and there are long periods when I cannot talk to you. On the level of the Logos, however, I talk to you constantly. When I am alone at home or up in the mountains or when I am travelling, I speak to you constantly.

I have neither wife nor children nor business interests in my life; I am free at every moment to think of you and all the other people on earth. To think of you and give you advice, light and encouragement and relieve you of some of your burdens. If you receive none of this, it is because you think that only physical speech counts. No; this is why I say that you must begin to practise here, when we are together: instead of waiting impatiently for the silence to end when it lasts a little longer than usual, learn to develop your antennae, to sense that your Master is thinking of you and of your future; try to divine what he is preparing for you, the future that he is trying to lead you to. There are things which he cannot express on the physical plane; things, even, that he has no right to put into words because there are some who would profane his words. This is why he utters them in the invisible world where only those who are prepared and sufficiently sensitive can receive them and use them for their spiritual progress.

11

A MASTER SPEAKS IN SILENCE

I

When we are here, together, you all wait expectantly for me to speak to you. But it would be quite unreasonable to think that I could ever satisfy all your desires. No one can talk for ever; there are too many reasons that make it impossible: it is tiring for the person who is talking and doubly tiring for those who are listening. The former becomes exhausted and the latter sated, and neither exhaustion nor satiety are to be recommended. To speak can be useful in one way and not to speak can be useful in another way. When someone talks to you, certain faculties of your brain are activated and, when he refrains from talking, other faculties are involved. For example, a woman sees that her husband is silent and thoughtful, so she watches him and tries to guess what is going on in his mind, where he has been, what happened to him, etc., and, in this way, she becomes more sensitive and perceptive.

Of course, it is good to develop qualities of this nature in respect to any human being, but how much more important to develop them in respect to an Initiate! Every day, during the summer conventions of the Brotherhood in Bulgaria, up near the seven lakes of Rila, we used to gather round the camp-fire with the Master Peter Deunov. We would sing a lot and the Master would sometimes talk briefly but, quite often, he would remain there in silence, meditating. At those times I would watch him and think to myself, 'What is he thinking about? Where is he?' In this way, I got into the habit of remaining in close touch with him and, little by little, I noticed that many of his thoughts, sensations and emotions came my way. I realized that he was silently teaching us. You will say, 'But you can't learn anything through silence; you can't hear anything!' On the surface of it, that is true, but it is the soul that receives something. A disciple's soul sees, feels and registers all that emanates from the soul and spirit of his Master. A disciple has no immediate perception of what his soul receives, but that is because it takes time before it can all be passed on to his brain and appear in his conscious mind. Sooner or later, however, it will turn up in the form of a thought, a discovery or a memory... and he will not even know where this new knowledge comes from.

Actually, without realizing it, every single human being contains within himself all the knowledge of the universe. It is buried deep down in his being and he can have no access to it for a very long time. It never stirs, never vibrates or manifests its presence in any way, for the conditions that would make this possible have not yet been achieved. You will ask, 'But how does this happen?' Oh, that is a very long story! Since that first day when human beings left the bosom of the Eternal Father and started to plunge deeper and deeper into matter, they have travelled a long way through time and space. In the course of this journey they have known many dramatic adventures and changes of fortune, gained a great deal of experience and acquired a great deal of knowledge. At the same time, however, they have lost much of their original light and knowledge. Or, rather, this original knowledge has gradually been buried under layers of dull, opaque matter and can be brought up to the surface again only under certain conditions.

Those who have already trodden the path of Initiation in a previous incarnation have less difficulty in rediscovering this knowledge. Sometimes, in fact, they only have to hear mention of certain ideas or to encounter an Initiate or a spiritual Master for a distant memory to awaken within them. It is as though the sound of those words or the presence of that being were sufficient to bring these memories back to them and, in many cases, they will not really need any further instruction or guidance. They are capable of guiding themselves; they are even capable of bringing up from the depths of their soul knowledge of things that their instructor has never revealed to them.

It is much more difficult, of course, for others. There are always a few who, when they hear certain ideas expressed, have a vague feeling that there is some truth in what they are hearing. They don't know that they already possess this knowledge but it is as though they heard the murmur of a distant voice urging them to accept it. And then there are the others — the vast majority, alas — who are left totally unmoved whatever they hear. Everything depends, therefore, on the degree of evolution a person has reached. However hard one tries, however persuasive one's arguments and however many philosophical systems one explains to people, they will never be convinced if they are not inwardly ready.

Human beings need to see with their eyes, to hear with their ears, to meet other people, to feel the shock of physical contact and to suffer. They are so inert, so numb and passive that, if they received no impulse from the outside world, if they were not shaken into wakefulness, they would never do anything. This is why Instructors and Masters are so necessary: because, thanks to the purity of their lives, thanks to their vibrations and the light and purity of their thoughts, they are capable of arous-

ing something within us. And, if they don't always
manage to do so, it is not because they are incapable
or weak, it is because we have allowed ourselves to
become buried under so many layers of leaden,
opaque materials that one wonders whether even
God Himself could get through to us.

As a matter of fact, the work of an Initiate is
similar to the work of Nature. How does Nature
work? She is constantly speaking to us and sending
us messages; not in words, of course: Nature
doesn't need words in order to speak to us. The sun
and the stars, forests and lakes, mountains and
oceans constantly speak to us and communicate
something of their own life, of their own secrets to
us. Even though we are not conscious of them, these
communications are recorded within us. In fact, it
is thanks to them that our sensibility is gradually
enriched and our understanding enhanced. We don't
know how this kind of understanding functions, but
it does. And an Initiate speaks to us in the same
way: by sending us currents and rays, by projecting particles in our direction. The silent words of
an Initiate are like a cosmic bombardment. But we,
of course, who are often so unaware as to be totally impervious to the communications of Nature, can
also be impervious to the silent communications of
an Initiate.

You will ask, 'What do we have to do in order
to vibrate in unison with an Initiate, in order to com-

municate with him in silence?' You have to make yourselves ready, that's all. You have to prepare yourselves. You have to make an effort to awaken the subtle world within you. Even if you have been unable to communicate with a particular Instructor because his face, gestures, attitude and words have failed to arouse a response in you, you can still work to prepare yourselves for another encounter in the future. For it is very likely that, one day, you will meet someone else with whom you will feel an affinity. If you have never made any effort to prepare yourselves, you will gain nothing from that encounter either.

II

When we are here together, meditating in silence, it is impossible for me immediately to forget about your presence and concentrate on my own work. You are with me; you are in my head and my heart as a unit, as my family and I speak to you, I explain things to you. Often, in fact, when I would like to stop and get on with my own work, I can't do it; I go on speaking to you. Sometimes, at these moments, without realizing it, some of you tune in to my thoughts and, one fine day, perhaps while you are out for a walk or writing a letter, you will suddenly be visited by an idea, an inspiration that comes to you like a bolt from the blue. Yes, because nothing is ever lost, not even a thought, for everything is alive. And this will become better and better if you continue to develop harmoniously and understand the real value of what we are doing here. When the time is ripe, each one of you will bring out into the light of day all the treasures stored up within you. This is why I say that you must make every effort progressively to reach a state of consciousness that will make it possible for us to gather simply in order to be together in silence and savour the divine life that fills the whole of space, the space in our soul and the space in the universe.

Once silence is established we are ready to receive the spirits of light and the revelations they can give us. It is not absolutely indispensable to talk in order to say something. I, too, can reveal things to you in silence. It is when we are no longer disturbed and distracted by noise that we are ready to hear subtler voices. And thought, even though inaudible, is a voice that can be heard and deciphered. It is in the midst of silence that the soul has a chance to grasp and comprehend spiritual realities and, for my part, I would much rather speak to your souls than to your ears.

In fact, in all sincerity, I must tell you that I have no great faith in the power of the word. In the present state of affairs, speech is one of the least productive ways of working. For thousands of years, human beings have talked and talked and talked but the Kingdom of God has still not come. There is nothing but talk. You will ask, 'But then, why do you continue to talk to us?' I talk to you in order to prepare the ground. But the truth is that I don't really believe that there is great power in the spoken word – nor in the written word, for that matter.

Look at all the books there are in the world!
And what have they ever changed? No, I am
looking forward to the time when you will be
capable of being together, like this, for a long time
without feeling the need for me to talk to you
physically. When will that day come? When you
have learned to be inwardly free and peaceful,
when you have learned to concentrate and do some
constructive work with the abundance of subtle
materials contained in silence. When you have
learned to do this you will feel how weak words
are compared to the strength and fulfilment that
silence can give you. If this is not possible for the
moment, if silence still fails to give you a fraction
of what words give you, it is because you yourselves
are not yet capable of perceiving the treasures it
contains.

To be sure, words have their uses: they can be
used to explain things, to give information and a
general orientation, but that is all. And they cannot even do this unless human beings are willing to
be persuaded. If they are not, words are powerless.
For the time being, therefore, I have to talk to you
because I know that it is still necessary; I can see
that it is necessary. But when, at last, words have
done their work and you are ready, we shall be able
to lose ourselves in the depths, the immensity, the
intensity of silence and you will see and feel for
yourselves that what you experience, then, is much

vaster and more powerful than anything you experience through words.

In the sanctuaries of the past, the Initiates knew enough about human nature not to overload their disciples with vast amounts of knowledge. This is the mistake of our modern universities: they oblige the students to learn such a mass of detail that they have no time to live or breathe. The Initiates said very little; they revealed a few essential truths and then left their disciples to meditate on them in silence, to steep themselves in them and learn to live them. Yes, the Initiates put all their love, all their soul and spirit into their words and their disciples received them, meditated on them and absorbed them into themselves. And they got far more nourishment from the life contained in their Masters' words than from the actual words themselves. But nowadays, particularly in the West, people have not developed the sensitivity that would enable them to discover the life contained in words and allow themselves to be nourished, strengthened and transformed by it. They count on the words themselves and, coldly and carefully, they record what they hear without experiencing anything vital. So it is to no purpose! All that hidden life which could enlighten, heal and resuscitate them goes to waste; they receive none of it. It is not your intellect but your soul and spirit that should be foremost here so that, thanks to only a few words, you will, one day, be capable of projecting yourself out into space.

I would much rather not talk to you very much... but that is for the future: the time is not yet ripe. You are not yet sufficiently developed, your faculties are not sufficiently sensitive to be able to perceive the thoughts of an Initiate who meditates and speaks to you in silence: you would gain almost nothing from it. A word can be grasped and understood on the physical plane because sound impinges directly on that plane. And this is not the case with thought. And yet, whether I am by myself or with you, I am constantly talking to you of things that cannot be expressed in words, things so lofty and divine that it is impossible to hear or comprehend them on the physical plane. 'But, surely', you will say, 'That's a waste of time. You're not achieving anything!' No, none of this is wasted because, although you are very rarely conscious of what you are receiving in this way, your psychic instruments are, nevertheless, receiving and recording it all. You don't know this, so you still have the impression that you have learned nothing but, one day in the future, when conditions are right, something that you have recorded in this way will suddenly rise to the surface of your consciousness and you will perceive it as a discovery, an illumination.

Believe me; it is quite true: I look forward with impatience to the day when I shall be able to speak to you in silence. At the moment, I know that there are very few of you who wish for this. You accept silence for a few minutes before and after my talks, but if our meetings were spent without a word being uttered, very few would be able to bear it. But this will come. When I speak to you with words it is as though I were obliged to stoop to a lower level, to restrict myself, whereas the fact of speaking to you without words triggers an upsurge of fantastic powers within me. Yes, this is far preferable for me; when I do this I can see the results. And I also see the results of talking to you with words.

Actually, I never stop talking to you in silence. At home or wherever I may be, I am constantly looking after you and giving you explanations and advice. You don't know this, you don't realize it but, sooner or later, you will benefit from it. In the meantime, try to understand, try to sense that the activity of a spiritual Master is much vaster and reaches much farther than anything you can imagine.

You are used to teachers and lecturers whose work can be seen and understood by anyone. But the activity of a spiritual Master is quite different; it is beyond our ordinary comprehension because it takes place, first and foremost, on the subtler planes of reality. Even if he also gives lectures, even if he also receives people who need encouragement and counselling, a spiritual Master acts essentially on the invisible plane, through his soul and spirit and his thought, the Logos. It is as though his whole being were pulverized and hurled out into space so that every particle of it might be used, as an element of light and peace, in the construction of the new life.

12

THE VOICE OF SILENCE
IS THE VOICE OF GOD

When I was young, in Bulgaria, I used to see people who came to see the Master Peter Deunov and, instead of listening to him and learning something from him, they would make a great display of their knowledge and talk about all the books they had read, etc. When this happened, the Master always behaved with surprising patience, listening to them and smiling gently. Sometimes he was simply unable to put in a single word. After a while, when these people finally realized that they were doing all the talking and that, if they did not stop, they would not learn anything, they kept quiet and allowed him to say something. And imagine their astonishment when they realized that they had learned more, after only a few minutes with him, than they had learned from several years of study! Simply because they had adopted a receptive attitude that made it possible for them to receive the Master's words.

A lot of people are like this: when they are in

the presence of someone who is superior to them
in competence, wisdom and nobility of character,
instead of being quiet and listening, they start chat-
tering about all kinds of things and even interrupt
him when he is speaking. That is not intelligent; you
gain nothing by behaving like that; on the contrary,
you lose. When you are in the presence of a superior
being, it is preferable to listen. Even if he does not
talk physically, if there is silence within you, he will
speak to your soul. When the Divine Spirit speaks,
Heaven and earth keep quiet and listen to His word,
for His word is a live, fertile seed.

Someone who is silent shows that he is ready to
listen, that is to say, ready to obey; when he speaks,
on the other hand, it shows that he wants to take the
initiative, to control and dominate. Silence, therefore, belongs to the docile feminine principle which
conforms to the masculine principle. If we have to
restore a climate of inner silence, it is because this
allows the Divine Spirit to do His work in us. As
long as we are obstreperous, defiant and anarchical,
the Spirit cannot guide us and we shall continue to
be weak and puny but, as soon as we manage to
achieve silence, we put ourselves in the hands of the
Spirit who guides us towards the divine world.

This receptive, 'passive' attitude must, on no account, be mistaken for sloth or inertia. It may seem,
at first sight, to be passive but, in fact, it is the
highest form of activity. It is the attitude of one

who, by means of a great deal of hard work, patience and sacrifice, has succeeded in establishing a climate of silence within himself and, thanks to that inner silence, can now begin to hear the voice of his own soul. And the voice of his soul is no other than the voice of God.

You must understand silence as the absolute condition, the essential matrix outside of which there can be no true word, no true revelation. In this silence you sense that messages begin to reach you, a voice begins to speak to you. It is this voice that forewarns, guides and protects you. If you cannot hear it, it is because you are making too much noise, not only on the physical plane but also in your thoughts and feelings. This is what is often called 'the voice of silence' – in fact, this is the title of several books of Oriental wisdom – and, if you want this voice to speak to you, you must give it the climate of inner silence it needs. When a yogi finally attains perfect inner silence, even to the point of halting all thought processes – for, when we think, even our thoughts make a noise – then he hears the voice of silence which is the very voice of God.

Just as we have a third eye in the middle of the forehead, we also have a third ear which lies at the base of the throat, on the level of the thyroid gland. In order to develop this third ear we have to learn to live in silence. The ears are linked to Saturn, the planet of solitude, inner stillness and introspection.

If the Initiates, hermits and ascetics of the past withdrew from the company of others and lived alone it was in order to listen to this inner voice. Like Saturn, they chose to be alone so that nothing should interfere with their concentration. Everybody knows that, when you need to reflect and decide something important, you go into a room alone and close the door behind you, because silence is a more favourable climate for making decisions. But even in that silence, we also know that there is often a great deal of noise, for man's inner sanctum is like a public forum in which crowds of people are constantly demonstrating and staging protest marches. It is no wonder that it is so difficult to hear the true answers to the questions we ask ourselves, the answers that come from Heaven, from the realm of silence.

Yes, however much we may want to isolate ourselves, we are never alone. We have so many 'tenants' living in us. Do you really believe that you are alone? That it is you who think, desire and decide? That the initiative is always yours? Well, if you do, you are mistaken. You are inhabited by a multitude of entities, in particular by the spirits of your family, both those of your family who are in the next world and those who are still alive on earth. They all have a foothold within you: all those who are addicted to drink, to their dishonest schemes for making money, to their pursuit of pleasure... they are all there, all trying to get you to satisfy their own perverted desires. And, in the long run, you give in to them − however silent your surroundings may be!

A disciple goes about things differently: he is not content to get away from external noises, he also endeavours to silence the shouts and threats and demands of the creatures within him. He makes them keep quiet and, in the great stillness within him he hears a voice, but a very soft, very faint voice.

This inner voice never stops speaking within each one of us, but it is so soft that we have to do a great deal of hard work before we are able to distinguish it amidst all the noise that is going on. It is as though, listening to a symphony orchestra, you tried to follow the delicate melody of a flute in the midst of all the noise of the big drums and double bass. It is not easy. It is something we have to learn to do: to listen for this gentle little voice and hear what it is saying to us. We have no difficulty in hearing the stentorian voice of the stomach clamouring to be fed or of the genitals clamouring for their prey, but when a tiny voice whispers, 'Be more patient. Control yourself. Make an effort', etc., our only response is, 'Oh, shut up!' And it is so easy to reduce this voice to silence. It is so gentle; it never insists.

You will say, 'But why is it like that? After all, God is almighty; surely He can use whatever means are necessary to make His voice heard?' That is true, but read the story of Elijah in the Old Testament. When Elijah had to flee for his life from Jezebel he went and hid in the desert for many days. Then the voice of God made itself heard. At first there was a tremendous wind which tore the mountains apart and broke the rocks in pieces, but God was not in that wind. Then there was an earthquake, but God was not in the earthquake. Then there was a fire, but God was not in the fire. Finally, after the fire, came the whisper of a still, small voice and God was in that whisper. Now you understand: God was neither in the hurricane, nor in the earthquake, nor in the fire; He was in that still, small voice. The voice of God makes no noise and we need to be extremely attentive in order to hear it.

The Prophet Jonah also heard the voice of God. It told him, 'Arise, go to Nineveh, and cry out against it; for their wickedness has come up before me.' But Jonah was frightened and did not at all want to go to Nineveh, so he ran away and boarded a ship bound for Tarshish. When they were at sea there was a great storm and the terrified sailors cast lots to see who was the cause of their troubles. The lot fell to Jonah who was thrown overboard and swallowed by a whale. Jonah remained for three days and nights in the whale's belly and, during that time, he thought about what the Lord had asked him to do and prayed to be delivered. Then Jonah promised the Lord that he would do his bidding, and the whale vomited him onto dry land. Like Jonah, he who is prevented from hearing the voice of the Lord by his own fears and vain desires often encounters a whale and has to spend several days in its belly until the clamour ceases and he is able to hear that voice. And how about you: how many whales have you already encountered in your life? Yes, there are whales of all sorts, sizes and colours!

If you were more attentive and had greater discernment, you would notice that, before you undertake anything important in life (a journey, a new job, an important decision), a soft little voice offers you advice. But you pay no attention; you prefer tumult and tempests. The being who is speaking to you would have to make a great deal of noise to get you to listen to him. If he speaks quietly, you don't listen. And yet, surely you must know that when superior beings speak to you they use few words and their voice is almost inaudible? Sometimes, when you have had an accident or something has gone wrong through your own fault, you will say, 'Yes, I had a sense that something was warning me not to go ahead, but it was so faint, so vague!' Exactly; and you did not listen to it because you preferred to listen to the loud, insistent voices that were leading you into error.

God speaks softly and without insistence. He says something once, twice, perhaps three times, no more. And intuition does the same; it never insists.

If you don't take the trouble to listen for it, if you fail to hear the voice of intuition because you are only capable of hearing loud noises, you will be constantly led astray. The voice of Heaven is extremely soft, gentle, melodious and brief and there are certain criteria that you must apply if you want to recognize it. Yes, it is possible to identify the voice of God because it manifests itself in three different ways: it engenders light within you; it fills your heart with a sense of expansion and warmth, a feeling of love, and it gives you a sense of liberation and makes you decide to act with nobility and disinterestedness. Pay attention to these things!

It sometimes happens that, when you have an important decision to make, you are confused and tormented because so many contradictory things crowd in on you. You feel that you are being pushed and pulled first in one direction, then in another and yet another. You cannot possibly see your way clearly in the midst of all this turmoil so you must postpone all decisions: whatever you decided in such conditions would inevitably be a mistake. It is much better to decide nothing until you are calmer and have regained your inner peace, for it is only then, when your thoughts and feelings fall silent, that you will receive an answer from your higher Self, from the Spirit. It is this silence that you need in order to make the right decisions, for it is this silence that is the source of lucidity, transparency and certainty.

Silence, peace, harmony; these are simply different expressions of the same reality. You must not think that silence is mute and empty. No; silence is alive and vibrant; it speaks, it sings. But we can hear it only when the thunder of the big drums ceases to reverberate within us. One day, thanks to contemplation, prayer and meditation, we shall hear the voice of silence. When, at last, peace comes to all the chaotic forces within us, silence will begin to grow and spread and wrap us in its marvellous mantle. Then a light will dawn in us and we shall suddenly feel that something very powerful hovers over us, that it is this that rules us, this silence from whose womb the universe was born and to which it will one day return.

13

THE REVELATIONS OF A STARRY SKY

Life in the modern world is organized in such a way that human beings are less and less in touch with nature. This is especially so in towns where it is often impossible even to see the sky or, if it is still visible, nobody ever thinks to look at it. People are so preoccupied and under so much stress because of their material concerns that their eyes turn more and more towards the earth. To be sure, people can see the sun but they don't look at it. And how many people ever take the time to look at the stars in the night sky?

I know that the conditions of modern life are not particularly conducive to contemplating the stars but still, it is something you should try to do whenever you have a chance, if only for a few minutes. In the silence of the night, imagine that you are leaving the earth and all its conflicts and tragedies behind you and becoming a citizen of the heavens. Meditate on the beauty of the stars and the magnificence of the beings that inhabit them. Little by little, as you rise mentally higher and higher, you will begin to feel lighter and freer and, above all, you will discover peace, a peace that gradually suffuses every cell of your being. Meditating on the Wisdom that created all these worlds and the beings of which they are a reflection, you will sense that your soul is putting out very subtle antennae which enable it to communicate with them. You will never forget such sublime moments, for the rest of your life.

Even after all these years, I still remember certain experiences I had when I was young, in Bulgaria. In the summer, when the Master Peter Deunov and the members of the Brotherhood camped in the Rila Mountains, I would sometimes climb up and spend the night at the top of Mount Musallah. I would wrap myself up in several blankets and, stretching out on my back, I would gaze up at the starry sky and try to link myself to the cosmic forces and entities of which the stars are only the physical aspect. I could not understand all that they said to me, but I loved them; my whole soul glowed with the wonder of them while I lay and looked at them until, without realizing it, I finally fell asleep. Sometimes it would snow a little during the night and I would wake up to find myself under a light covering of snow. But that never worried me: I was happy!

Those were the years in which I discovered the extraordinary peace that floods one's being when one spends the night on a mountain. I found myself transported to regions in which I felt and understood that the only activity that really matters in life is to become one with the cosmic Spirit that animates the universe. The slightest little thing in the everyday lives of human beings torments them and sets them at each others' throats. Their consciousness has such a narrow field of vision that they think there is nothing more important than their petty cares, ambitions, love affairs and quarrels. They cannot see the immensity, the infinite reaches of the heavens over their heads which, if only they would lift their eyes to it, would permit them to break the bonds that restrict them and breathe a purer air. Don't be like that; don't deprive yourself of all the different opportunities that arise to lighten the burden of daily life.

Reflecting on infinity and eternity, you will begin to feel that you are floating above all contingencies, that nothing can touch you any more. Distress, sorrow and bereavement no longer have the power to trouble you, for a new consciousness awakens within you and enables you to feel and judge things differently. This state of consciousness which is new to you is that of the Initiates and great Masters: whatever happens to them, whether they are deprived of their rights, betrayed or injured, none of it really affects them; they are above it all. Unfortunately, most human beings cannot understand this; they are accustomed to stagnating on the lowest levels of thoughts and feelings and it is this that makes them so weak. Not knowing how to disentangle themselves, they are perpetually victimized by the negative conditions that they themselves have allowed to take root in them.

Believe me, it is important to learn to use all possible occasions to rise above such a terribly mediocre life. And the star-filled sky in the silence of the night is one such occasion which invites us to forget our earthly affairs for a few minutes and think of other worlds in which other, more highly evolved creatures live in harmony and splendour. All the things we worry so much about mean nothing to them; they are too tiny, too insignificant. You will say, 'What? Are you saying that famine and mass murder and all the other cataclysms we experience are insignificant? But they're frightful!' Yes, they are frightful but, in the eyes of Cosmic Intelligence, they are hardly worth mentioning. In the eyes of Cosmic Intelligence, the only events that matter are those that affect the soul and the spirit.

When the sky is clear at night, therefore, get into the habit of gazing at the stars and drinking in the peace that flows so sweetly from a starry sky. Put yourself in touch with each star and you will find

that they respond and speak to you like living, intelligent souls. Try to pick out one with which you
feel a special affinity and link yourself to it, imagine
that you go and talk to it or that it comes and talks
to you. The stars are very highly evolved souls. If
you listen to them, you will find the solution to
many of your problems and feel more peaceful and
enlightened.

All the great Initiates learned by contemplating
the night sky; when their souls were in communion
with the stars, these powerhouses of inexhaustible
forces, they received messages from them which they
then transmitted to men. We have to learn to read
the stars as though we were learning to decipher a
sacred scripture of which the stars are the letters.
And this cannot be done all at once; it is only after
a long time that we begin, little by little, to understand what they have revealed. In fact, even I am
only now beginning to understand some of the
things that the starry skies whispered to me in the
silence of the night. My soul received and recorded
those messages and they have been stored safely
away ever since.

When I watched the twinkling of the stars, sending signals of light through space to each other, it
seemed to me, too, that they were at war with each
other – but a war of light and love. And now I
know that war will always exist in the universe, for
the principle of Mars will always be there (that is,

the need to compete, the need to prove oneself
stronger than others), but the nature of war and its
manifestations will be different. Weapons of death
and destruction will be replaced by weapons that
shoot rays of light and love. This is what the stars
taught me: that it is possible to fight a war of love
and light.

14

A SILENT ROOM

If you ask a sage to describe God he will say nothing; his only response will be silence, for silence alone can express the essence of the Deity. Yes, to say what God is is not enough; and to say what He is not is not enough either. It is true to say that God is love, wisdom, power and goodness, but it is also true to say that these words fall far short of the divine reality; they are incapable of encompassing anything of the infinity, eternity or perfection of God. We cannot know God by talking or hearing others talk about Him; we can only know Him by plunging into the depths of our own being and entering that innermost region: the region that is silence.

Every human being possesses certain subtle centres in his body – known in the Hindu tradition as chakras or lotuses – which serve as channels of communication with the spiritual world. But these centres cannot be animated and made to function in the midst of the noise and bustle of everyday life.

There have always been a certain number of people
– hermits, anchorites, sadhus, etc. – who, in their
desire to escape from the demands and aggressions
of the outside world, chose to withdraw into the
depths of a forest or into a desert. Some of them,
in their desire to cut themselves off from all inter-
course with the outside world, went even further and
tried to silence their five senses and put them out
of action altogether. With this in mind, they dug
holes in the ground just big enough for them to get
into and there they took refuge. By putting their
senses to sleep in this way, they were able to achieve
an inner state of absolute silence. As there was
nothing for them to see, hear, feel, taste or touch,
they succeeded in piercing the opaque screen that
cuts man off from true reality. When I was in India
I met some of the rare beings who had experienced
this and, even though I knew a lot about it before
I met them, they taught me a great deal about the
power of true silence, that silence which, alone,
makes it possible for all our spiritual centres to start
vibrating and functioning.

True silence is not simply the absence of noise.
True silence is above wisdom, above music; it is the
most luminous, the most powerful, the most
beautiful of worlds; it is the centre from which stem
all creations. True silence is God Himself. And we
must frequently make contact with this silence, frequently immerse ourselves in it and try, even, to stop

thinking. Once you achieve this silence the most extraordinary peace will flood your being; you may even hear God speaking to you, for it is only in silence and peace that God is willing to speak.

To immerse oneself in silence, therefore, is an activity that lies beyond the scope of the five senses, beyond feelings, even beyond thought. To attain the realm of silence is to float in an ocean of light, to live in the intensity and abundance of true life. People sometimes experience this silence after great suffering or a great upheaval in their lives. It is as though the shock of their suffering catapulted them beyond themselves into the realm of the Entity known to Initiatic Science as the Silent Watcher.

The fact is, though, that most people, even when they have had such an experience, spend most of their lives at the outer fringes of their being. For them, the inner life goes no further than the realm of the heart and intellect; no further, that is, than the astral and mental planes. And on these planes, of course, there is a lot of bustle and activity. What with all our desires, sensations, passions, sorrows and self-seeking motives and ambitions, there is always plenty for us to see and hear and busy ourselves with. But on a deeper level all this turmoil changes nothing; man is not transformed by it. If he is to be transformed in depth and discover something essential, he cannot remain on that level, he must rise to the Causal, Buddhic and Atmic planes.

Everybody has their ordinary, run-of-the-mill thoughts and feelings; there is no need to make an effort to achieve that, you only have to let yourself go. But if you want to cultivate feelings inspired by divine love and know higher states of consciousness, you have to make an effort. And the efforts you have to make are disinterestedness, detachment and self-abnegation. These are the preliminary conditions that have to be present before you can hope to enter the realm of silence.

Some of you might say, 'But this silence you are talking about, this world that lies beyond the world of thoughts and feelings is nothingness, the void. You seem to be telling us to throw ourselves into this void. It's terrifying!' From one point of view, it is true, you could call it the void. But don't be afraid, I have never said that you should throw yourself into it just like that, before you were ready for it. Why should I be less intelligent or more cruel than a mother bird? What does a mother bird do? She keeps her newly hatched chicks in the nest for as long as necessary and, only when they are fully fledged and capable of flying, does she push them out of the nest; not before. And this is what I do for you: I don't push you out into the void before you are ready for it. I simply show you, in advance, the work that lies before you and the means you must use to do that work; that's all.

In any case, emptiness, the void, is not an end

in itself. To empty oneself is to learn to rid oneself of all the foreign elements that prevent us from being in contact with the divine world and receiving its blessings. So many men and women are like bottles that are full! There is no possibility of pouring anything more into them: they are filled to the brim with unhealthy desires, false ideas and prejudices. It never occurs to them to empty themselves so as to replace darkness with light, ugliness with beauty, disorder with order. When it comes to replacing a worker, an employer, a husband or a wife, everybody has the skills required, but if you talk to them about replacing error with truth or a fault with a quality, they look at you in astonishment.

So it is true that to achieve silence is, as it were, to achieve a void, an emptiness within oneself, and it is in this emptiness that one receives fullness. Yes, because, in actual fact, there is no such thing as a void. If you pour the water out of a container it will be filled with air; if you empty out the air, it will be filled with ether. When you empty the matter from a container in an attempt to create a void, the matter that you get rid of is always replaced by something subtler. In the same way, when we reject inferior thoughts, feelings and desires, it is the light of the spirit that rushes in to fill our emptiness and, when this happens, we see, we know.

Silence is the highest region, the summit of our soul and, when we reach this region, we enter into cosmic light. Light is the quintessence of the universe; everything we see around us, as well as everything we cannot see, is suffused and impregnated with light, and the goal for which we are striving in attempting to attain silence is precisely this: to fuse into one with that living, potent light that permeates the whole of creation.

If it is possible in your house or flat, try to set aside a room, however small, as an oasis of silence. Decorate it with beautiful colours and a few symbolic or mystical pictures and dedicate it to the Heavenly Father, the Divine Mother, the Holy Spirit and the Angels and Archangels. Never let anyone, including yourself, go into it if they are not capable of achieving inner silence in order to listen to the voices of Heaven. In this way, you will be giving your soul and spirit a chance to blossom and to receive many Heavenly blessings which you can then shower on all the creatures around you. If you learn to maintain the right attitude, something harmonious will emanate from the walls and objects in the room and attract entities of light, for harmony is their nourishment. If you are sad or discouraged, you will only have to go into that room and, within a few minutes, you will feel completely restored, for it will be full of kind friends who ask nothing better than to console and help you.

But, as you go about making this silent room ready, you must be conscious of the fact that, at the same time, you are making ready a silent room within yourself, in your own soul and heart. In this way, wherever you may be and however tumultuous your circumstances, you will always have that silent room into which you can go to find peace and light. We live at one and the same time in both worlds — the visible and the invisible, the material and the spiritual — and this is why it is good to have this silent room both in oneself and outside oneself, and to protect it from all malign influences.

I know that what I am saying is not for everybody; it is only for those who, in spite of all they have received in life, are not satisfied, who still feel that something essential is lacking. So, I leave it to you to decide for yourselves. But, once you make up your mind to follow the path of silence, you must not worry about how long it will take you to reach the end. The only thing that is essential is your decision to tread this path and to persevere.

By the same author

Izvor Collection
TABLE OF CONTENTS

205 – SEXUAL FORCE OR THE WINGED DRAGON

1. The Winged Dragon – 2. Love and Sexuality – 3. The Sexual Force is Essential for Life on Earth – 4. Pleasure : I – Do not Seek Pleasure for it Will Impoverish You – II – Replace Pleasure with Work – 5. The Dangers of Tantric Yoga – 6. Love without Waiting to be Loved – 7. Love is Everywhere in the Universe – 8. Spiritual Love is a Higher Way of Feeding Ourselves – 9. A High Ideal Transforms Sexual Energy – 10. Open Your Love to a Higher Path.

206 – A PHILOSOPHY OF UNIVERSALITY

1. What is a Sect ? – 2. No Church is Eternal – 3. The Spirit Behind the Form – 4. The Advent of the Church of St. John – 5. The Foundations of a Universal Religion – 6. The Great Universal White Brotherhood – 7. For a Universal Notion of the Family – 8. Brotherhood, a Higher State of Consciousness – 9. The Annual Conventions at the Bonfin – 10. The Universal Dimension of All Our Activities.

207 – WHAT IS A SPIRITUAL MASTER ?

1. How to Recognize a True Spiritual Master – 2. The Necessity for a Spiritual Master – 3. The Sorcerer's Apprentice – 4. The Exotic Should not be Confused with Spirituality – 5. Learn How to Balance the Material and Spiritual Worlds – 6. A Master is a Mirror Reflecting the Truth – 7. A Master is There Only to Give Light – 8. The Disciple and His Master – 9. The Universal Dimension of a Master – 10. The Magical Presence of a Master – 11. Identification – 12. 'Except Ye Become as Little Children...'

208 – THE EGREGOR OF THE DOVE
OR THE REIGN OF PEACE

1. Towards a Better Understanding of Peace – 2. The Advantages of Unity amongst Nations – 3. Aristocracy and Democracy – 4. About Money – 5. The Distribution of Wealth – 6. Communism and Capitalism – 7. Towards a New Understanding of Economics – 8. What Every Politician Should Know – 9. The Kingdom of God.

Down...' − 7. The Calming of the Storm − 8. The First Shall Be Last − 9. The Parable of the Five Wise and the Five Foolish Virgins − 10. 'This is Life Eternal, that they Might Know Thee the Only True God'.

218 − THE SYMBOLIC LANGUAGE OF GEOMETRICAL FIGURES

1. Geometrical Symbolism − 2. The Circle − 3. The Triangle − 4. The Pentagram − 5. The Pyramid − 6. The Cross − 7. The Quadrature of the Circle.

219 − MAN'S SUBTLE BODIES AND CENTRES
the Aura, the Solar Plexus, the Chakras...

1. Human Evolution and the Development of the Spiritual Organs − 2. The Aura − 3. The Solar Plexus − 4. The Hara Centre − 5. Kundalini Force − 6. The Chakras: The Chakra System I. − The Chakra System II. Ajna and Sahasrara.

220 − THE ZODIAC, KEY TO MAN AND TO THE UNIVERSE

1. The Enclosure of the Zodiac − 2. The Zodiac and the Forming of Man − 3. The Planetary Cycle of Hours and Days − 4. The Cross of Destiny − 5. The Axes of Aries-Libra and Taurus-Scorpio − 6. The Virgo-Pisces Axis − 7. The Leo-Aquarius Axis − 8. The Fire and Water Triangles − 9. The Philosophers' Stone : the Sun, the Moon and Mercury − 10. The Twelve Tribes of Israel and the Twelve Labours of Hercules in Relation to the Zodiac.

221 − TRUE ALCHEMY OR THE QUEST FOR PERFECTION

1. Spiritual Alchemy − 2. The Human Tree − 3. Character and Temperament − 4. Our Heritage from the Animal Kingdom − 5. Fear − 6. Stereotypes − 7. Grafting − 8. The Use of Energy − 9. Sacrifice, the Transmutation of Matter − 10. Vainglory and Divine Glory − 11. Pride and Humility − 12. The Sublimation of Sexual Energy.

222 – MAN'S PSYCHIC LIFE:
ELEMENTS AND STRUCTURES

1. Know Thyself – 2. The Synoptic Table – 3. Several Souls and Several Bodies – 4. Heart, Mind, Soul and Spirit – 5. The Apprenticeship of the Will – 6. Body, Soul and Spirit – 7. Outer Knowledge and Inner Knowledge – 8. From Intellect to Intelligence – 9. True Illumination – 10. The Causal Body – 11. Consciousness – 12. The Subconscious – 13. The Higher Self.

223 – CREATION: ARTISTIC AND SPIRITUAL

1. Art, Science and Religion – 2. The Divine Sources of Inspiration – 3. The Work of the Imagination – 4. Prose and Poetry – 5. The Human Voice – 6. Choral Singing – 7. How to Listen to Music – 8. The Magic Power of a Gesture – 9. Beauty – 10. Idealization as a Means of Creation – 11. A Living Masterpiece – 12. Building the Temple – Postface.

224 – THE POWERS OF THOUGHT

1. The Reality of Spiritual Work – 2. Thinking the Future – 3. Psychic Pollution – 4. Thoughts are Living Beings – 5. How Thought Produces Material Results – 6. Striking a Balance between Matter and Spirit – 7. The Strength of the Spirit – 8. Rules for Spiritual Work – 9. Thoughts as Weapons – 10. The Power of Concentration – 11. Meditation – 12. Creative Prayer – 13. Reaching for the Unattainable.

225 – HARMONY AND HEALTH

1. Life Comes First – 2. The World of Harmony – 3. Harmony and Health – 4. The Spiritual Foundations of Medicine – 5. Respiration and Nutrition – 6. Respiration: i. The Effects of Respiration on Health – ii. How to Melt into the Harmony of the Cosmos – 7. Nutrition on the Different Planes – 8. How to Become Tireless – 9. Cultivate an Attitude of Contentment.

226 – THE BOOK OF DIVINE MAGIC

1. The Danger of the Current Revival of Magic – 2. The Magic Circle of the Aura – 3. The Magic Wand – 4. The Magic

Word — 5. Talismans — 6. Is Thirteen an Unlucky Number — 7. The Moon — 8. Working with Nature Spirits — 9. Flowers and Perfumes — 10. We All Work Magic — 11. The Three Great Laws of Magic — 12. The Hand — 13. The Power of a Glance — 14. The Magical Power of Trust — 15. Love, the Only True Magic — 16. Never Look for Revenge — 17. The Exorcism and Consecration of Objects — 18. Protect Your Dwelling Place.

227 — GOLDEN RULES FOR EVERYDAY LIFE

1. Life: our most precious possession — 2. Let your material life be consistent with your spiritual life — 3. Dedicate your life to a sublime goal — 4. Our daily life: a matter that must be transformed by the spirit — 5. Nutrition as Yoga — 6. Respiration — 7. How to recuperate energy — 8. Love makes us tireless — 9. Technical progress frees man for spiritual work — 10. Furnishing your inner dwelling — 11. The outer world is a reflection of your inner world — 12. Make sure of a good future by the way you live today — 13. Live in the fullness of the present — 14. The importance of beginnings... etc.

228 — LOOKING INTO THE INVISIBLE
Intuition, Clairvoyance, Dreams

1. The Visible and the Invisible — 2. The Limited Vision of the Intellect, The Infinite Vision of Intuition — 3. The Entrance to the Invisible World : From Yesod to Tiphareth — 4. Clairvoyance : Activity and Receptivity — 5. Should We Consult Clairvoyants ? — 6. Love and Your Eyes Will be Opened — 7. Messages From Heaven — 8. Visible and Invisible Light: Svetlina and Videlina — 9. The Higher Degrees of Clairvoyance — 10. The Spiritual Eye — 11. To See God — 12. The True Magic Mirror: The Universal Soul — 13. Dream and Reality — 14. Sleep, an Image of Death — 15. Protect Yourself While You Are Asleep — 16. Astral Projection While Asleep — 17. Physical and Psychic Havens — 18. The Sources of Inspiration — 19. Sensation is Preferable to Vision.

Editor-Distributor

Editions PROSVETA S.A. – B.P. 12 – 83601 Fréjus Cedex (France)

Distributors

AUSTRIA
MANDALA
Verlagsauslieferung für Esoterik
A-6094 Axams, Innsbruckstraße 7

BELGIUM
PROSVETA BENELUX
Van Putlei 105 B-2548 Lint
N.V. MAKLU Somersstraat 13-15
B-2000 Antwerpen
VANDER S.A.
Av. des Volontaires 321
B-1150 Bruxelles

BRAZIL
NOBEL SA
Rua da Balsa, 559
CEP 02910 - São Paulo, SP

BRITISH ISLES
Prosveta
The Doves Nest
Duddleswell
Uckfield
East Sussex TN22 3JJ

Dorset SP7 8PL

CANADA
PROSVETA Inc.
1565 Montée Masson
Duvernay est, Laval, Que. H7E 4P2

GERMANY
EDIS GmbH
Daimlerstr.5
D - 8029 Sauerlach

GREECE
PROFIM MARKETING Ltd
Ifitou 13
17563 P. Faliro
Athens

HOLLAND
STICHTING
PROSVETA NEDERLAND
Zeestraat 50
2042 LC Zandvoort

HONG KONG
HELIOS – J. Ryan
P.O. BOX 8503
General Post Office, Hong Kong

IRELAND
PROSVETA IRL.
84 Irishtown – Clonmel

ITALY
PROSVETA Coop. a r.l.
Cas. post. 13046 – 20130 Milano

LUXEMBOURG
PROSVETA BENELUX
Van Putlei 105 B-2548 Lint

NORWAY
PROSVETA NORDEN
Postboks 5101
1501 Moss

PORTUGAL
PUBLICAÇÕES
EUROPA-AMERICA Ltd
Est Lisboa-Sintra KM 14
2726 Mem Martins Codex

SPAIN
ASOCIACIÓN PROSVETA ESPAÑOLA
C/ Ausias March n° 23 Principal
SP-08010 Barcelona

SWITZERLAND
PROSVETA
Société Coopérative
CH - 1808 Les Monts-de-Corsier

UNITED STATES
PROSVETA U.S.A.
P.O. Box 49614
Los Angeles, California 90049

VENEZUELA
J.P. Leroy
Apartado 51 745
Sabana Grande
1050 A – Caracas

PRINTED IN FRANCE IN JUNE 1990
EDITIONS PROSVETA Z.I. DU CAPITOU,
B.P.12, 83601 FRÉJUS CEDEX
FRANCE

– N° d'impression: 1812 –
Dépôt légal: Juin 1990
Printed in France